Conquering

Your

Unseen Enemies

Conquering Your Unseen Enemies

How Jesus Sets You Free

Gary V. Whetstone

Gary Whetstone Publishing

New Castle, Delaware

Gary Whetstone Publishing
P.O. Box 10050
Wilmington, DE 19850 U.S.A.
PHONE: 1(302) 324-5400
FAX: 1 (302) 324-5448
WEB SITE: www.gwwm.com
E-MAIL: info@gwwm.com

Conquering Your Unseen Enemies is a revised and updated work adapted from Gary Whetstone's book *Victory in Spiritual Warfare* (ISBN 0-88419-243-1), which Creation House first published in 1990.

All scripture quotations, unless otherwise indicated, are taken from the HOLY BIBLE, NEW INTERNATIONAL VERSION®. NIV®. Copyright © 1973, 1978, 1984 by International Bible Society. Used by permission of Zondervan Publishing House. All rights reserved.

Scripture quotations marked (AMP) are taken from The Amplified Bible, Old Testament. Copyright © 1965, 1987 by The Zondervan Corporation. The Amplified New Testament, copyright © 1954, 1958, 1987 by The Lockman Foundation. Used by permission.

Scripture quotations marked (NKJV) are taken from the New King James Version. Copyright © 1982 by Thomas Nelson, Inc. Used by permission. All rights reserved.

Scripture quotations marked (KJV) are taken from the King James Version of *The Holy Bible.*

ISBN 0-9664462-2-4

For though we live in the world,
we do not wage war as the world does.
The weapons we fight with
are not the weapons of the world.
On the contrary,
they have divine power to demolish strongholds.
We demolish arguments and every pretension
that sets itself up against the knowledge of God,
and we take captive every thought
to make it obedient to Christ.
2 Corinthians 10:3-5

Finally, be strong in the Lord and in his mighty power.
Put on the full armor of God
so that you can take your stand against the devil's schemes.
For our struggle is not against flesh and blood,
but against the rulers,
against the authorities, against the powers of this dark world
and against the spiritual forces of evil in the heavenly realms.
Therefore put on the full armor of God,
so that when the day of evil comes,
you may be able to stand your ground,
and after you have done everything, to stand.
Stand firm then,
with the belt of truth buckled around your waist,
with the breastplate of righteousness in place,
and with your feet fitted with the readiness
that comes from the gospel of peace.
In addition to all this, take up the shield of faith,
with which you can extinguish
all the flaming arrows of the evil one.
Take the helmet of salvation
and the sword of the Spirit,
which is the word of God.
Ephesians 6:10-17

Contents

Part 5: Appendix

Part 1

Testimony

of a

Modern Demoniac

1
Who Is this Madman on the Loose?

Wham! Wham! Bang!

"What's that?" The pounding from the front porch startled Tom Craig.

"Somebody's trying to break open the door!" Tom's wife, Linda, shrieked in panic.

The wood molding gave way in a shower of splinters as a booted foot crashed against it. The door flung open. Silhouetted against the yellow glare of the streetlight stood the hulking figure of a madman.

"I own this house! It's mine!" roared the intruder. His eyes flashed as they roamed from one side of the room to the other, pausing briefly to glare at Tom.

"What? Who are you?" Tom almost choked in dread at the sight of the frightful apparition. As his eyes focused on the figure, Tom noticed the wild, intense blue eyes, then the tangled reddish-brown hair and the bushy beard. The intruder looked like a barbarian, a pirate! However, this pirate wore the ragged T-shirt, torn jeans, and matching denim vest typical of the motorcycle gangs that roamed the Wilmington, Delaware, neighborhoods.

"Shut up!" The bearded thug demanded, as he strode across the threshold. He was less than twenty years old, but he stood six inches taller than Tom. "I said this is my house!" The madman repeated, swinging his arm in an arc. He pointed to the furniture, a piece at a time. "That's my couch! That's my chair! That's my table! That's my lamp!"

Tom could not believe what was happening. Questions flooded his mind: *Who is this monster? Why has he invaded my house? He must be insane—maybe strung out on drugs—obviously dangerous. He's bigger than I am. Can I stop him—get him out of here—without him killing us?*

Horrible fear gripped Linda. Her petite body began to shake—98 pounds of trembling terror. Beads of sweat popped out on her forehead. She was dumbstruck—paralyzed with fear.

The intruder turned to look at Linda, leering with lust. "That's my wife, and I'm going to have her!" He lurched toward the terrified woman.

Tom sprang forward. "No, you don't!"

The madman's foot flashed upward, catching the shocked husband in the stomach. Tom dropped to his knees and rolled in a ball on the floor, gasping in pain.

The intruder was powerful beyond his size. He grabbed Linda, threw her onto the couch, and pounced on her, covering her screaming mouth with his grimy hand. His intent was clear.

Fear and rage produced a rush of adrenaline that spurred Tom into action. He struggled to his feet, hobbled to the hall closet, jerked open the door and grabbed his shotgun. Then Tom turned toward the attacker and yelled, "Leave her alone, or I'll kill you!"

The madman roared, leaped to his feet and rushed at Tom, ignoring the shotgun. The two grappled, cursing, slugging, and kicking. Tom finally succeeded in clubbing the intruder with the shotgun, momentarily stunning him.

"For God's sake, call the police, Linda!" Tom ordered. She

jumped up from the couch and stumbled down the hallway.

The bearded man roared in pain, shook his head, and sprang to his feet to attack the householder once more. Tom dodged his onrushing charge. The attacker tripped over the ottoman and crashed into the fishtank, splattering its ten gallons of watery contents all over the wall and carpet.

Tom hurled himself onto the water-soaked madman. They squirmed, cursed, and struggled together. Tom finally pinned the assailant's arms to his sides.

"Had enough?" Tom asked.

"Yeah, yeah," grunted his opponent.

Tom eased his grip. With a surge of strength the intruder wrenched free and ran out the door into the chilling September night. Tom grabbed the shotgun and raced after him.

"Oh, no, you don't! You're not getting away!" shouted Tom. He swung the gun above his head as he closed in on the fleeing man.

Thud. The gunstock made contact, and the assailant was down for the count.

When the fallen man opened his eyes, he was staring up the length of the shotgun, the muzzle jammed inside his mouth. "Don't move a muscle, sucker, or I'll blow your brains out!" he heard Tom growl.

Then the intruder snarled, "Go ahead and kill me!" His face filled with rage. Pinned against the fence, the thug tried in desperation to force Tom to pull the trigger and end this tormented existence. He kicked Tom in the groin, but Tom somehow maintained his pose and did not pull the trigger.

Within minutes, a special S.W.A.T. team of four heavily armed policemen arrived at the scene. They handcuffed the madman and dragged him, kicking and screaming, into one of their cruisers.

I was that madman.

The names of Tom and Linda Craig are fictitious, but the events of that night in September 1971 really took place. Due to my deranged condition, some of the details remain fuzzy, though I can still remember the taste of that shotgun barrel. The screaming desire to conquer or die is as vivid today as it was then.

Incredibly, I am completely normal now—sane, rational, and reasonable. In fact, I am the pastor of a fast-growing church in my hometown of New Castle, Delaware. Imagine that! I am a pastor in the same area in which these events took place!

What caused my insane, violent behavior in the first place? It's a story that will help you to understand the severity of the prevalent drug problem and the culture of violence that has invaded our schools, cities, and rural communities. What caused my recovery? It's a story of the Lord's grace that will amaze you and bring glory to our miracle-working God.

2
Destroy the All American Boy?

In 1968, I was the typical all American boy. My high-school grades were good. I served as president of the Student Council. A wiry 120 pounds, I excelled in sports and was captain of the freshman football team. I also held several backstroke records for the swim team and was number two in the state tennis championship. My future looked very bright—until one fateful, snowy day.

Sledding is a wonderful winter activity, and my friends and I enjoyed racing down the slopes. I did not intend to slide out of control into the path of an oncoming car, but it happened. When I slammed head-on into that automobile, I tried to stop myself by stretching out my right arm, but the impact drove my arm through my back.

At the hospital, the doctors did everything possible to repair the damage. They removed chest muscles and sewed them around my back. Although the doctors saved my arm, its movement was limited. That meant the end of my swimming and football careers. It also meant the end of tennis competition. Although I could still play slightly, I had lost my overpowering serve and forehand forever.

Only in the area of academics did I continue to perform well. Unfortunately, however, that did not mean much to my peers or me. My friends at Conrad High School in Delaware were looking for the athletic type. I did not fit into their social circle and, as a result, I became insecure. I lost interest in all sports and forfeited my position as president of the Student Council. Most of all, I lost my identity—who I believed I was. My grades slipped from A's and B's to C's and D's. By the tenth grade, this handicap completely had destroyed my self-image and reason for living. Although I grew to be five-feet-ten-inches tall, I saw myself as half a person.

My brother, Wick, was six years older than I was. By this time he was 22 and president of the Pagans' motorcycle club, with several hundred members ranging from Wilmington to South Philadelphia. He became my idol, and the Pagans were my best friends and "protectors."

Most of the Pagans rode Harley-Davidson "hogs," but I was breaking in a lighter-weight motorcycle. The hogs were too hefty for me to handle comfortably, but no other part of the Pagans' lifestyle was too heavy for me. Drugs, sex orgies, gun dealing, and violence—I bought it all. According to my twisted thinking, conforming to their way of living would gain me respect within the group. I did not hesitate to live outside the law.

Money was easy. Guns, violence, drugs, and sex always provided the lifestyle we demanded. If the Pagans wanted something, we had it, or could get it—from assault guns to kilos of the most powerful South American drugs available. Our trade thrived, and the price was right—but with danger. I always carried a .38-caliber pistol and, frequently a derringer depending upon whom I expected to see. During our many drug runs, I enjoyed and became proficient in the use of certain automatic weapons and explosives.

Since I had easy access to drugs, I was always "high." Soon, I was using up to five hits (doses) of LSD a day. Little by little, my mind deteriorated. Only while living in a stupor of alcohol and hard drugs did I find stability. Gradually, I became filled with aggression, fear, and hatred. By the time I reached the eleventh grade, many of my gang-member friends were in prison or victims of murder. Death and violence surrounded me. I was paranoid. My emotional pendulum swung from a solitary lifestyle to wild drug parties. I did not understand how to relate to a normal society. At times I went into uncontrollable rages and frequently could no longer distinguish right from wrong. I experienced terrifying hallucinations, heard weird voices, and carried out the voices' violent mandates.

My parents were at a total loss about what to do. They committed me to the Delaware State Hospital for psychiatric treatment and drug rehabilitation. However, when the doctors released me, I resumed my pattern of drug abuse and lawless lifestyle. My parents committed me again, then again, and again. Four times I was in and out of the mental hospital before I finished eleventh grade! By this time, my mother had turned to heavy drinking. Both her boys were confined—one in prison and the other in a mental asylum.

Somehow I managed to graduate from high school in 1971, but my behavior became thoroughly antisocial. My obsession caused me to believe I possessed things that I did not own. For example, one night, while driving my van through a local neighborhood, I saw a pickup truck with two nice outside mirrors on it. I stopped my van, opened my tool chest, and started to remove the mirrors from the truck.

A passerby paused to ask, "What are you doing?"

"These are *my* mirrors!" I screamed, cursing. "They fit *my* truck!" I finished removing them and calmly drove away.

This bizarre behavior persisted for several months. Finally, it culminated about six blocks from my parents' house. There, I kicked in the door of "Tom and Linda Craig's" home, terrifying the occupants with claims that I owned the house, its contents, and even the wife.

This violent escapade resulted in the court making me a ward of the state. Deranged and unable to be with other people, I spent most of my hospital time in isolation. Life in a padded cell is horrible beyond imagining. An insane person often will tear off his clothes, bang his head against the walls, and attempt to mutilate himself. Sometimes, he even will smear his feces all over the cell. Guards shove the patient's meals through a slot in the door, and often a person in isolation will use the plates for a toilet. When hosing out the filth from the cell, guards must restrain the patient physically. That was how I existed.

During this time, the psychiatrists analyzed my mental condition. In their final evaluation, they declared me hopelessly insane. Afterward, the state committed me to the mental institution for the rest of my life. There was no hope of recovery!

The hospital authorities contacted my parents and confronted them with the findings. Since the doctors considered my condition to be hopeless, they proposed putting me into an extremely dangerous experimental program (which is now illegal in the United States). This treatment would include boring a hole in my head, then subjecting me to intense electrotherapy or powerful shocks to delay certain control centers of my brain. The officials predicted that these procedures would eliminate my violent behavior, erase all my memory, and cause me to become manageable.

However, the consequences would be severe. They would reduce my mind to that of a three-year-old child, and I would lose control over my speech, motor coordination, and all memory. Also, I would lose the ability to control my bladder and bowels. Basically, the doctors were asking my parents for permission to reduce their son to a guinea pig for scientific research.

My parents agreed to the experiment. Perhaps it was because I had put them through Hell on earth and the doctors had explained there was no hope for recovery. They signed the waiver stating that if the state of Delaware killed or permanently maimed me, they would hold no legal recourse against the state. Usually after people received this treatment, they never were seen again.

The top psychiatrist ordered me to attend a meeting with my parents to explain the scheduled experiment. Most days I was bound in fetters. These were heavily woven fabric restraints that held my arms and legs as firmly as handcuffs and leg irons, but without inflicting the cuts and bruises that metal manacles cause. However, on this day, I was free from restraints in the psychiatrist's office. As the doctor began his explanation to me, I lurched into another uncontrollable rage. Hurling myself at him, I attempted to destroy the doctor. The guards instantly sprang into the room and subdued me. I soon found myself back in isolation. That Wednesday marked the end of any further attempt at explanation or family contact.

In two days, the procedure would begin. It would take several weeks to complete, because the doctors did not want to give the entire treatment to me at once. They said a slower process would enable me to maintain my motor coordination. Possibly, I still would be able to walk, but I would not retain my memory or the ability to speak. Ultimately, that would be my future.

Or would it?

11

Jesus said:

For just as the Father raises the dead and gives them life, even *so the Son gives life* to whom he is pleased to give it.

John 5:21

Jesus was about to give life to me!

3
What Is "Born-Again"?

The local news media followed the story of my life. To most who saw the account, the reports held little significance: *There goes another one off to the asylum,* they probably thought. However, to some of my former high-school classmates, the news was tragic. I had befriended none of them. In fact, I was surly and strange to most of my class. Yet, I did have one friend, and we had a thread or two in common.

That friend attended a Baptist church. He had shared with his pastor, Ron Hayden, what had befallen me. What could they do? Pray? Yes, they did that, but he wanted the pastor to contact me. After a midweek service one Wednesday night, my friend urged Pastor Hayden to visit me. After all, ministers can visit patients in the state mental hospital, while ordinary youth cannot.

So on the next day, Thursday—just one day before I would become a vegetable—Ron Hayden waited in the mental hospital's solarium to see me. Why had it been so simple to arrange? Maybe the authorities decided that one last contact with a religious leader was the least they could do for a person they were about to reduce to a vegetable. It was like "last rites."

The guards led me from isolation, my hands and feet strapped in restraints, and took me to meet the preacher. I must have been a shocking, pathetic sight. I shuffled on unsteady legs, and my shoulder-length red hair and tangled beard stuck out through my inmate's garb. To quiet me, the doctors had heavily sedated me, causing spittle to drool from the corner of my mouth. Since I was not a threat while in this kind of stupor, the guards freed me from the restraints for this visitation.

When I made my sluggish entrance, the pastor sat down. Then, looking directly at me, I clearly heard him speak. The words cut through the fog that clouded my mind. "Gary," he asserted, "I know exactly what's wrong with you."

The visitor caught me by surprise! Never had anyone said that to me. All the psychiatrists, psychologists, and psychoanalysts had been unable to determine the cause of my affliction. Instead, they placed labels on me such as "paranoid" and "psychotic." (Now, labeling a disorder may bring some satisfaction to a doctor, but it does not offer much hope to the patient.) Suddenly, this preacher was claiming that he could identify my problem. I was ready to listen.

"It's the power of sin," Hayden said simply. "The power of sin is going to kill you." I thought he knew of the procedure that I was to receive starting the next day.

Even in my drugged state, his words pierced me.

"You can have a new life! All you have to do is believe in your heart that Jesus Christ died for you and rose from the dead," the preacher continued. "Then, confess with your mouth that Jesus is Lord."

That's all I heard, but it was all I needed to hear.

I do not know what the pastor thought about me that day. Did he see me as a hopeless case or as a genuine prospect for salvation? Did he present the Gospel invitation in a mechanical way? Or did he experience a profound sense of anointing? I do not know. I only remember that this visitor said what I needed to hear. Somehow the Lord gave power to his words, and they penetrated my deepest self.

I fell to my knees on the floor, sobbing and calling on Jesus to come into my heart. Yes, at that moment, I believed He died for me. Yes, I believed He rose from the dead. Yes, I confessed with my mouth, "Jesus is Lord!"

After a few minutes, I regained control of myself and stood up. Everything was different. Somehow, despite the overload of drugs, my mind was clear and rational. I looked at the preacher through tear-filled eyes. "Do you know what happened to me?" I asked.

"Yes," he said. "You were born-again." However, the pastor did not attempt to explain what this meant.

"What is that?" I asked.

"Well, now you are saved!" His answer did not help me to understand. "Well, our time is up," he added. "May God bless you." That was his final reply.

Then, he left.

The next day, the doctors had scheduled me for the procedure that would reduce my mind to that of a three-year-old child. All hope had disappeared. Or had it? Did God have other plans?

4
"Run! Run!"

After Ron Hayden's visit, the guards once again wrapped me in restraints. Now, I had a different problem: I was a normal person imprisoned in a mental hospital, with doctors who were unknowingly about to destroy me! I tried to convince everyone that I was sane, but no one would listen. When I returned to my isolation cell, I beat on the walls to get someone's attention. They ignored my apparently routine behavior. After all, this was ordinary behavior for me.

Finally, the next day, the staff took me to see the head psychiatrist. I tried to explain my spiritual experience, but the doctor said, "Gary, I'm sorry. With the tremendous level of instability you are displaying, it is very common for someone to imagine a religious encounter. This is merely another manifestation of the completely incurable problems you are experiencing. It does not matter if it is religion you get involved in or something else. These are crutches for someone like you. Until you become reoriented to live successfully in society, none of these will work. We will proceed as scheduled."

At that point, I became so enraged with the doctor that I attacked him! Now, this kind of behavior may be shocking. After all, I had been born-again supposedly. Born-again people don't act violently, do they? Well, I did. Yes, I was born-again, but I did not know how to release anger. My spiritual training was zero.

17

Following the assault, my doctor hit the panic button, and immediately the security guards came to take me away. On my chart, the physician simply wrote, "No change." That was the end of our meeting. I realized at this point that my next stop was debilitating electrotherapy.

Or was it?

On this fateful day—another snowy day—my life was about to change again forever.

As the guards led me back to the isolation area, I heard a different voice, commanding me, "Run! Run!" Hearing voices was not uncommon to me, but this voice was like none I ever had heard.

I questioned the incredulous thought: *Run? Where can I go? It's snowing outside, and I have no shoes, only socks. The guards will see my state hospital uniform—and the locked doors stand in my way!*

However, I stopped in the middle of the hallway to look around. The windows had heavy chain screens on the inside with bars on the outside. Two guards watched me through porthole windows on each side of the hall.

Again I asked myself, *Where can I run?*

Suddenly, my attention was drawn to a nearby door. It was unbolted, and the unlocked chains merely hung there!

Once more I heard the word, "Run!" At that moment I felt a surge of energy, and I took off running.

There is no natural explanation for what happened next. The guards on station did not try to stop me. Yet they physically stood, watching as I escaped. Did God blind their eyes?

I darted through the door and headed toward the commissary, where the more trusted patients loitered. I ran through yelling, "I'm on the run! I'm on the run!"

The patients lifted their voices and pounded their fists on

the tables, shouting in unison: "Run! Run! Run! Run!" The sound echoed in the commissary hall as two of the braver patients ran with me.

"Take my coat!" one yelled.

"Here are my shoes!" the other one shouted.

As they tossed their possessions to me, I stopped to put them on quickly. The heavy Army pea coat was too large, and the big shoes fit my feet like boats.

I continued running. Not too far in the distance, the guard shack loomed in my path. I realized that anyone with long, red hair and a beard, state hospital pants, shoes that did not fit, and an oversized coat definitely looked like an escapee. Although fear gripped me, I slowed down, tucked my hair and beard into my coat, and walked past the guardhouse as though nothing were wrong. I walked as if I belonged outside those gates, because I did belong out there. I was sane again! Thank God!

When the Baptist pastor had left the day before, I had not understood what had happened to me. Now, I know that I had become God's child on that Thursday. The moment I became born-again, all God's promises began to work in my life. One promise after another I began to experience! He has delivered me from the kingdom of darkness into the kingdom of light.

Giving thanks to the Father, who has qualified you to share in the inheritance of the saints in *the kingdom of light.*

For he has *rescued [delivered] us from the dominion of darkness and brought us into the kingdom of the Son* he loves,

in whom we have redemption, the forgiveness of sins.

Colossians 1:12-14

God literally had rescued me from the mental hospital and electrotherapy apparently by unlocking that door and blinding all the guards!

You see, God will not allow the enemy to tempt you beyond what you can endure. With each test, He always provides a way of escape so you can bear it.

> There hath no temptation taken you but such as is common to man: but God is faithful, who will not suffer you to be tempted above that ye are able; but will with the temptation also make a way to escape, that ye may be able to bear it.
>
> 1 Corinthians 10:13 (KJV)

After I passed the guardhouse and reached Route 40, I ran as fast as I could. However, I soon realized I could not get far on foot before the police caught up with me. So I decided to find a ride.

Straight ahead I saw a man in his pickup truck waiting at a traffic light. He was the most likely candidate to take me home. So I ran to the truck, opened the passenger door, and jumped inside. "Take me home!" I commanded.

The man stared at me. "You look like you're in trouble," he said.

"No, not me," I calmly replied. "Everything's all right. I'm doing great!"

Of course, he had to have known that I was from the asylum. How could I hide this fact, since the label on my clothes read, "Property of the State Hospital"?

However, instead of shoving me out the car, the man drove me home. I asked him to drop me off a few blocks away from my parents' house, because I expected him to call the police.

How do you explain a complete stranger's willingness to transport a man who is obviously an escapee from a mental hospital? It does not make sense—unless you add God to the equation. He definitely can make people act contrary to their normal courses of behavior. Our God is faithful even if we do not know it!

When I reached my parents' house, no one was home. I broke in, got some clothes and money, and took the keys to my old van. Then, I drove day and night nonstop to Florida.

Again I realize that my conduct may perplex a church-going, law-abiding reader. Supposedly, I was a born-again follower of Jesus. Yet, I had escaped from the mental hospital, coerced a stranger into giving me a ride, and broke into my parents' home. In my spiritual infancy, these actions appeared perfectly logical. Breaking the law certainly is not acceptable behavior for new converts. However, I am simply reporting what I did. Possibly a better way to view God's interaction with us is that He reaches us where we are—not where religious people think we should be.

While I was in Florida, my brother discovered that some of our previous associates were planning to kill me! They believed I had turned state's evidence against several of them, whom the police had arrested recently. These were the people I thought I could trust, and now they wanted to murder me. (Isn't that like the devil and his crowd?) The police had issued an all-points bulletin on me, so I could not go anyplace or see anyone without the danger of murder or capture.

My older brother contacted a lawyer in Delaware. He did everything possible to have the state overturn its judgment against me, but to no avail. If I returned, I faced the certainty of becoming a vegetable.

I'm tired of running, I thought. *How will I ever get out of this mess alive?* Since I had run with fugitives before, I knew what it was like to hide from the law. With no other apparent choice, I ordered new identification documents and began to accept that my life would never be normal again. Yet, that day on a street corner in Fort Lauderdale, I prayed a second time. "Jesus, if this experience with You is real, then I want to return to Delaware and get a release from this hospital treatment. I want my freedom back to live a normal life." Suddenly, an awesome peace came over me. I knew that God would work it all out!

As I drove back into my hometown, a policeman, whom I had known since my childhood, stopped me. "Gary!" the officer called as he looked into the van, using his flashlight.

I gazed back and greeted him. He definitely was not the person I had wanted to meet at three o'clock in the morning. I pleaded with the officer, "Look, whatever you do, don't arrest me. I'm going to park my van and sleep in it for a few hours. In the morning, my parents have agreed to take me back to the mental hospital."

The policeman let me go, and miraculously did not turn me in!

The next morning, I returned to the state hospital, as I had promised the policeman. When I arrived, the officials looked at me very strangely. Their expressions appeared to say, *I cannot believe this guy is back!*

I explained my requests. "Please don't give me any drugs," I begged. "Put me in an open, mixed (male-and-female) ward, and give me every psychological test available. I will prove to you that I am sane!"

The Bible says:

For God hath not given us the spirit of fear; but of

power, and of love, and of a *sound mind.*

2 Timothy 1:7 (KJV)

I did not know this verse then, but I realized that my mind was sound. Since I had returned under my own free will without fear, the doctors decided to grant my requests.

After three months passed, the psychiatrists had completed all the tests and they could not find anything wrong! They even compared my previous tests with those I had just taken. It was as if the results belonged to two different people!

Now, because of the absolutely remarkable changes they saw, the doctors concluded something *else* must be wrong with me. (I believe the Holy Ghost healed me physically and mentally.) Because of this confusion about my test results, the doctors decided that I must have a brain tumor! To solve this new prognosis, they gave me two choices. The first option was to let them cut off the top of my head to do a craniotomy—exploratory brain surgery—in search of the "tumor." The other choice was to have a pneumoencephalogram, a special X-ray of my head. Since I did not like the idea of having the top of my head cut off and walking around bald, I agreed to have the X-ray.

After completing the X-ray, the doctors still could find nothing wrong. They even told me, "We cannot figure out what is wrong with you, because there is nothing wrong with you!" So they released me from the hospital.

I was free to live in society. However, I still did not fit in at church, work, or anywhere "on the outside."

5
Stand on Solid Ground

When I left the state mental hospital, I was ignorant of the Word of God and still walked after my own fleshly desires. I did not know how God expected His sons to live. Yet, I was His son. Although I soon was baptized in water, I did not "fit in" with Christians. My actions and thoughts still were wild.

I did not know anyone to confide in. Since I was not a reputable person, no one would listen to me. Nor did anyone offer to help me experience more freedom. Obviously, I could not go back to my old friends. They thought I was strange, wondering: *What's all this religious stuff that Gary is talking about?* I felt stranded. My spiritual life was at a standstill. I knew I was losing my grip on Christ as I started to fall away from the Lord. Because I did not know how to fix my problems, they began to grow constantly!

All this time, I was dating my future wife. Then, in May 1972, Faye and I married. In 1973 our son, Eric, was born, and in 1974 Laurie was born.

Soon, the bottom dropped out again. As one match can destroy an entire building, so can a careless mistake change one's direction in life. I smoked only one joint of marijuana at a small party during the summer of 1974, and the result was total chaos. The same confusing spirits that had attacked me in the past suddenly began to harass me once again. By October 1975, Faye and I separated. Later, because of these problems, we divorced. I did not know what to do. Again, my life was falling apart at every level.

In the meantime, God had been at work in my mother's life. She had been attending a Wednesday afternoon Bible study sponsored by a group of Catholic charismatic believers. She had become born-again and then baptized in the Holy Spirit.

One day my mother told me, "Gary, you've got demons in you."

I thought, *Gee, Mom, thanks for the good news.*

"You have a choice," she continued. "You can go back to the state hospital, or you can get those demons cast out of you."

Since I already had been to the state hospital and knew what the plans were there, I opted for the second choice!

I decided to attend a church service at a nearby independent charismatic church. At the meeting, the Lord baptized me in His Holy Spirit, and I started speaking in other tongues. I did not understand what was happening, but it was terrific!

However, my troubles were far from over. I had some unseen enemies that I needed to conquer.

By this time, I already had attempted suicide twice. I want you to know that even born-again people can commit suicide. Satan will deceive and confuse anyone, if he can. I was a believer! I may not have been a very strong believer, but I still believed. I had Jesus in my heart and the baptism in the Holy Spirit. Yet, I was experiencing bouts of terrible depression due to the divorce.

I vividly recall my third attempt at suicide. It was in the fall of 1975. In the midst of a deep depression, I drove my Volkswagen onto a railway crossing. There, I waited on the tracks for the train to slam me into eternity. I told God that only He could save me from death. Although I knew that Satan was trying to kill me again, I did not know how to stop him. I yielded to my unseen enemy's plans of destruction. Suddenly, I heard a voice deep within me proclaim, "You shall not die, but live, and declare the works of the Lord." I did not realize it at the time, but this is a verse from the Bible!

I shall not die, but live, and declare the works of the LORD.

Psalm 118:17 (KJV)

Soon, I heard the rumble of the approaching train. Anticipating the crash, I shut my eyes and braced myself for certain death. The train whizzed by, but nothing happened! I was still sitting there unharmed in my Volkswagen. Amazed and puzzled, I opened my eyes to see why I was still alive. The huge engine had just rushed past my parked car on a second set of tracks that were only a few feet away! Later, I learned that the train had been rerouted temporarily that night to the other tracks during some repair work.

God had saved my life, once again, but for what reason?

Thoroughly shaken, I drove to my ex-wife's mobile home. I told her what had happened and begged her to take me to a private mental clinic to prevent another suicide attempt. I was desperate.

Near the end of my two-week stay in the clinic, a local charismatic pastor, knowledgeable in the ministry of deliverance, came to see me at my request. This pastor, who also had a degree in clinical psychology, recognized that my battle was not psychological. He said it was due to the activity of demons. These were my enemies, but I had never known they existed. I was in a war—but did not know it—and I had enemies that I could not see! It is no surprise that I was in captivity.

The pastor arranged for a Holy Spirit-filled layman to join with him in casting out the demons that had been driving me to self-destruction.

Following this time of ministry, I stayed in the clinic two days. By the time I left, God had delivered me from the tormenting spirits. It was then that I realized something important: My mother had been right. Satan had originated the problems that I had experienced for all those years. He was the source—my unseen enemy. Now, God had shown me how to conquer the devil.

After God delivered me, I began to fast, pray, and claim His Word for the restoration of my marriage. He honored my faith in His Word. Soon, in January of 1976, Faye became born-again and filled with the Holy Spirit. In July of 1976, we remarried each other.

For the next four years, I focused my attention on gaining new insights into the Word of God and on devoting quality time to my family. I now treasure my wife and our two beloved children, Eric and Laurie, and my grandchild, Isaiah.

During this period, tragedy struck. My mother died after a long illness, and six months later my father had a heart attack and died suddenly. Overnight, Faye and I became guardians of my 15-year-old brother, Chris. Thank God for the knowledge of His Word that produces stability in our lives. No longer would the winds of adversity blow me off my foundation in Christ.

I left my job as a welder and went into business. God's blessing was evident. The business thrived. For the first time, I felt that I was standing on solid ground. For three years, I prospered through my great responsibility in the business community. We built our lives, indeed, upon a good foundation—Christ, the Solid Rock. God led me to begin several businesses, which prospered. Still we remained firm and stable upon our foundation in Christ. Our business ventures eventually grew into multimillion-dollar corporations. Faye and I were active members of a local church and assumed leadership roles in that church body.

In 1983, while Faye and I enjoyed a wonderful vacation in Acapulco, Mexico, I sensed the Lord guiding me in a new direction. He asked me to sell my businesses and enroll in Rhema Bible Training Center in Broken Arrow, Oklahoma. I obeyed. Near the end of my training, I sensed the Lord's direction again. He called me to travel to Indonesia with my family. This was before we began serving in the pastorate of what is now known as Victory Christian Fellowship in New Castle, Delaware. (This church began with only three people!)

6
"Declare the Power of God!"

Faye and I enjoyed ministering in Indonesia for six weeks with our children. Eric was 11, and Laurie was 10. We traveled with a national evangelist who interpreted for us. The most profound benefit of our evangelistic effort was not what happened to the crowds but to the preacher. There, God transformed my ministry.

While we were in that country, the Spirit of the Lord asked me, "What is your Gospel?"

I answered, "My Gospel proclaims that Jesus Christ is the Son of God, who died for the world." Although my response was not wrong, I sensed that God wanted to communicate something beyond what I currently perceived.

"The Good News does not simply *tell about* something," the Spirit of the Lord said to me. "The Good News *is* something. The Good News is the power of God."

Although I had attended Bible school and had visited many churches, I had never realized this before. I knew Romans 1:16:

> For I am not ashamed of the gospel of Christ: for it is the power of God....
>
> Romans 1:16 (KJV)

I had read that passage at least a hundred times. Yet, when the Holy Spirit spoke to me that day, I received a different understanding.

The Lord repeated, "I have given Good News to you. That Good News is the power of God."

My spirit began to ponder this profound Word from the Lord. Immediately the Holy Spirit led me to various verses in the Scriptures. First, I read:

> "Whoever believes and is baptized will be saved, but whoever does not believe will be condemned.
>
> "And these signs will accompany those who believe: In my name they will *drive out demons*; they will *speak in new tongues*;
>
> "they will *pick up snakes* with their hands; and when they *drink deadly poison*, it will not hurt them at all; they will *place their hands on sick people, and they will get well.*"
> Mark 16:16-18

Before travelling to Indonesia, I had been casting out devils and speaking in tongues for several years. So I did not have a problem with these doctrines. However, when I reached the rest of this passage, I had to work at believing those events would happen.

Next, I read the following two verses:

> After the Lord Jesus had spoken to them, he was taken up into heaven and he sat at the right hand of God.
>
> Then the disciples went out and preached everywhere, and the Lord worked with them and confirmed his word by the signs that accompanied it.
> Mark 16:19-20

After I finished reading this passage, the Lord spoke to me

again. "I want to give an undeniable witness to this nation," He said, "that I am alive from the dead."

Although the Indonesians in general have good moral standards and appear stable, most of them did not know my God. Indonesia is an Islamic nation. The major problem with Islam is the people cannot prove their god is alive.

Over and over, I heard in my spirit, "The Good News you have for this nation is the power of God." I was beginning to understand. Suddenly, the Lord commanded me, "Declare the power of God! Declare the power of God!"

I thought, *Declare the power of God? How do I declare the power of God?*

The Holy Spirit replied, "Just demonstrate it." Then, He reminded me of what Paul had said:

And my speech and my preaching was not with enticing words of man's wisdom, but in demonstration of the Spirit and of power:

That your faith should not stand in the wisdom of men, but in the power of God.

1 Corinthians 2:4-5 (KJV)

As I meditated on those words, I thought, *Paul had a different message.* I remembered one example. In his letter to the Romans, Paul declared that Jesus Christ was the Son of God with power:

Concerning his Son Jesus Christ our Lord, which was made of the seed of David according to the flesh;

And *declared to be the Son of God with power,* according to the spirit of holiness, by the resurrection from the dead.

Romans 1:3-4 (KJV)

Paul did not believe in a compromising gospel. Never did he teach that sometimes God can perform certain works, while at other times He fails to do so. For example, Paul did not preach that sometimes God heals, but at other times He does not. This would mean that God's power within the believer varies from day to day. No, Paul knew that God's power never changes.

> Jesus Christ the same yesterday, and to day, and for ever.
>
> Hebrews 13:8 (KJV)

Paul also did not preach that God's power varies depending upon the believer. God is no respecter of persons:

> Then Peter opened his mouth, and said, Of a truth I perceive that God is no respecter of persons.
>
> Acts 10:34 (KJV)

Therefore, since "God does not show favoritism" (NIV), the same omnipotent power of God is available to all believers always.

When I finished pondering everything the Holy Spirit had taught me, I was ready to preach! My next meeting was very different from all others. As I began to preach, my interpreter immediately noticed something different. When we progressed deeper into ministry, she told me, "I have never said words like these before."

"Don't worry about it," I assured her. "Just repeat what I say."

She responded, "What if He doesn't do it?"

"Well," I answered, " then our God isn't who He says He is."

You see, if you preach the Gospel of Jesus, you first must settle this matter in your heart. How? Simply believe that God's

Word is true and that, as you speak it, He will demonstrate Himself and His promises. In other words, when we preach His Word in faith, we can *know* that signs will follow! Remember, God says that He watches over His Word to perform it.

> Then the Lord said to me, "You have seen correctly, for *I am watching to see that my word is fulfilled."*
>
> Jeremiah 1:12

If God cannot manifest His power, then we have an impotent religion, like Islam. If God cannot bring the results He promised to us, then this Gospel is merely a figment of our imaginations, and there is no power for life after death. God forbid! No, the Jesus I know is the same Paul knew. Let's read Romans 1:3-4 now in the *New International Version:*

> Regarding his Son, who as to his human nature was a descendant of David,
> and who through the Spirit of holiness was declared with power to be the Son of God by his resurrection from the dead: Jesus Christ our Lord.
>
> Romans 1:3-4

This Jesus rose from the dead in resurrection power and walked with the apostles, proclaiming the Word with signs following. The apostles then went on to preach the same Jesus Christ, the Son of God, with power.

The Bible says that the same Spirit that raised Christ from the dead also dwells in us as believers:

> But if the Spirit of him that raised up Jesus from the

dead dwell in you, he that raised up Christ from the dead shall also quicken your mortal bodies by his Spirit that dwelleth in you.

Romans 8:11 (KJV)

Today, we can go about, like the apostles. We can preach that same Jesus—the Son of God—with power to perform signs, wonders, and miracles.

The book of Acts records the reason God has poured the Holy Spirit upon us. Jesus said:

> But ye shall receive power, after that the Holy Ghost is come upon you: and ye shall be witnesses unto me both in Jerusalem, and in all Judaea, and in Samaria, and unto the uttermost part of the earth.

Acts 1:8 (KJV)

This verse says we shall be "witnesses" of Jesus. This means we will produce evidence, which proves to the world that Jesus Christ rose from the dead.

One piece of evidence that I have is the account of my life. I literally saw the power of God transform my life. I know what happened in me. This is my evidence. Today, I stand as a testimony to the resurrection power of Jesus Christ. Now, when I tell my testimony, according to Revelation 12:11, I defeat my unseen enemy by the Blood of Jesus:

> And they overcame him by the blood of the Lamb, and by the word of their testimony.

Revelation 12:11a (KJV)

Jesus Christ is alive! He is present right where you are. He has power and authority to free you from every shackle, burden, and weight in your life, today. He is there to deliver you from your limits and conquer your unseen enemies. Will you allow Him to set you free?

In the Acts of the Apostles, we read:

> *And with great power gave the apostles witness of the resurrection of the Lord Jesus:* and great grace was upon them all.
>
> Acts 4:33 (KJV)

What evidence did the apostles have that Jesus Christ was alive from the dead? It was POWER! The apostles had the Holy Spirit within them as evidence. However, the world needed a *visible* demonstration of God's power to verify that Jesus was alive.

The apostles' Jesus is the same Son of God who is present right where you are. He has not changed one bit! Today, He still heals the sick. In fact, I have seen tumors the size of basketballs disappear in people's clothing, as a result of God's power! Deaf people instantly have regained their hearing! I have seen God create limbs and flesh right in my hands. Thousands of people have become born-again and thousands have received the Holy Spirit. This is all because I prayed in the Name of Jesus!

Yes, we have power in the mighty Name of Jesus. We will discuss this in further detail later. However, I want you to know what happened when God raised Jesus from the dead.

> Wherefore God also hath highly exalted him, and given him a name which is above every name:
> That at the name of Jesus every knee should bow, of things in heaven, and things in earth, and things under

the earth;

And that every tongue should confess that Jesus
Christ is Lord, to the glory of God the Father.

Philippians 2:9-11 (KJV)

God exalted Jesus. He gave to His Son a Name to which all
"things in heaven...in earth, and...under the earth" would be
subject. Now, when we use His Name, we have the same
authority as Jesus Himself.

Then Jesus came to them and said, "All authority in
heaven and on earth has been given to me."

Matthew 28:18

Then he [Jesus] called his twelve disciples together,
and gave them *power and authority over all devils,* and to
cure diseases.

And he sent them to preach the kingdom of God, and
to heal the sick.

Luke 9:1-2 (KJV)

God wants you to know that His life within you will triumph
over all the works of the enemy. Today, if you are a Christian,
you can use that mighty Name of Jesus anytime. Through Jesus'
Name you can see blind eyes open, crippled people walk, and
demon-possessed people set free.

There is a testimony inside you that God wants you to let
out. He does not want the fear of failure or others' opinions to
limit you. This new-creation life is not a people-pleaser. It is a
God-pleaser. Your new nature wants you simply to say, "Father,
is that what You want me to do? Okay, I'll do it."

My family and I returned from Indonesia with a transformed ministry. Those six weeks marked a turning point in my life.

On August 15, 1984, we launched our church, Victory Christian Fellowship in New Castle, Delaware. That day, only three people attended in addition to my family. Today, thousands of people are present each week. Local outreaches bring more than 50,000 to the church for ministry each month. We now have 140,000 square feet of buildings.

Today, I serve as Senior Pastor of Victory Christian Fellowship. Also, the Lord has used me to establish the School of Biblical Studies and the School of Ministerial Training, which are outreaches of Gary Whetstone Worldwide Ministries. I speak and minister in mass open-air crusades with more than 100,000 in attendance, schools of ministry, and spiritual-warfare conferences around the world. I teach, lead mass prayer meetings, relate my own experience of demonic oppression, and train people to cast out demons effectively and win in spiritual warfare. I show them how to conquer their unseen enemies. I write these not as my fleshly accomplishments, but for the glory of God. It is a testimony of the life-changing power of my omnipotent Heavenly Father God; my living resurrected Savior, Jesus Christ; and my ever-present Comforter, the Holy Spirit.

Remember, "God is no respecter of persons." What He did for me, He wants to do for *you!*

In the remainder of this book I will share with you some of the lessons I have learned. We will examine in detail many of the verses mentioned in this chapter. In the following sections, you will learn who you are in Christ, and how to confront Satan and the work of evil spirits. Then, you, too, can conquer your unseen enemies!

Part 2

Know

Who You Are

in Christ

7
Understand Your Inherited Sin Nature

To discover and fully recognize who you are in Christ, you first must realize what your Savior saved you from. Jesus Christ came to destroy the sin nature of fallen mankind. What is the sin nature? How did you receive it? What is eternal death? In this chapter, we will discuss the answers to these questions and more. You will catch a glimpse of the new life you can expect as a Christian.

Please read this chapter very carefully. It contains a powerful revelation that many believers and even preachers do not grasp fully! Wrong doctrine in this area has caused many in the Church to believe the devil's lies and live in defeat. Unless you understand this foundation, you will not have the confidence in Christ to conquer your unseen enemies.

Two Kinds of Death

According to the Bible, man can die two kinds of death. One is physical death, the separation of the physical body from the soul and the spirit of man. In this death, the body stops functioning, the person is dead, and his loved ones have a funeral.

However, man's life does not end there. As we will read shortly, the Bible explains that after physical death, human beings continue to exist spiritually. We either experience for all eternity spiritual life with God (the One from whom our spirits came) or spiritual death with the devil (our unseen enemy). This kind of death permanently separates the human spirit and soul from God's presence, causing the person to live eternity in Hell.

You must know where you stand. Will you receive eternal life in the resurrection of the just, or will you be damned to Hell for all eternity? The book of Revelation describes this resurrection and the following events of the White Throne Judgment:

> Then I saw a *great white throne* and him who was seated on it. Earth and sky fled from his presence, and there was no place for them.
>
> And I saw *the dead, great and small, standing before the throne,* and books were opened. Another book was opened, which is the book of life. *The dead were judged* according to what they had done as recorded in the books.
>
> The sea gave up the dead that were in it, and death and Hades gave up the dead that were in them, and each person was judged according to what he had done.
>
> Then death and Hades were thrown into the lake of fire. The lake of fire is the *second death.*
>
> If anyone's name was not found written in the book of life, he was thrown into the lake of fire.
>
> Revelation 20:11-15

Jesus also explained the judgment, saying that He will separate the "sheep" from the "goats":

> "When the Son of Man comes in his glory, and all the angels with him, he will sit on his throne in heavenly glory.
>
> "All the nations will be gathered before him, and he

will separate the people one from another as a shepherd separates the sheep from the goats.

"He will put the sheep on his right and the goats on his left.

"Then the King will say to those on his right, 'Come, you who are blessed by my Father; take your inheritance, the kingdom prepared for you since the creation of the world.'

"Then he will say to those on his left, 'Depart from me, you who are cursed, into the eternal fire prepared for the devil and his angels.'

"Then they will go away to eternal punishment, but the righteous to eternal life."

Matthew 25:31-34, 41, 46

"But the cowardly, the unbelieving, the vile, the murderers, the sexually immoral, those who practice magic arts, the idolaters and all liars—their place will be in the fiery lake of burning sulfur. This is the *second death.*"

Revelation 21:8

When a person who is not a child of God physically dies, he experiences the tragic "second death." This, however, was not God's original plan for man. God had a higher calling for His precious creation, but man fell. Let's read the story of man's Fall as it unfolded in the Garden of Eden.

Three Trees in the Garden of Eden

As we will read in Genesis, God created Adam and planted a garden for him to dwell in:

And the LORD God formed the man from the dust of the ground and breathed into his nostrils the breath of life, and man became a living being.

Now the LORD God had planted a garden in the east, in Eden; and there he put the man he had formed.

And the LORD God made *all kinds of trees* grow out of the ground—trees that were *pleasing to the eye and good for food.* In the middle of the garden were *the tree of life* and *the tree of the knowledge of good and evil.*

Genesis 2:7-9

Notice, there were three kinds of trees in the Garden of Eden:

- One kind bore fruit for food.
- The second was the tree of life.
- The third was the tree of the knowledge of good and evil.

Now, before God created Eve, He gave an important commandment to Adam about the trees:

And the LORD God commanded the man, "You are free to eat from any tree in the garden;

"but *you must not eat from the tree of the knowledge of good and evil, for* when *you eat of it you will surely die.*"

Genesis 2:16-17

The phrase *you will surely die* means that in the process of dying, you will die. By eating from this tree, man would begin to die, and this would end in his eternal death.

Because God is omniscient (all knowing), He predicted in

verse 17 above that Adam would eat the forbidden fruit. However, not only did God give the prophetic revelation of Adam's Fall, He also foretold how He would restore man back to Himself. We will read this later. The way back would be through Jesus' death and the preaching of the cross.

Eve's Creation

Then, finding "no suitable helper" (Genesis 2:20, NIV) for Adam amongst the animals, God created Eve. However, instead of forming her from the dust as He had created Adam, God made the woman from Adam's side. He put Adam into a deep sleep, took out a rib, and closed the flesh thereof. From that rib, God created a new person. Notice, the woman did not come into the earth like Adam, who came from nothing:

> Through faith we understand that the worlds were framed by the word of God, so that things which are seen were not made of things which do appear.
>
> Hebrews 11:3 (KJV)

Remember, God made Eve *after* placing Adam in the Garden of Eden. Therefore, Eve received her Maker's commandments about the trees through her husband, Adam. This is important.

Eve's Temptation with the Knowledge of Good and Evil

As recorded in the third chapter of Genesis, the devil—using the body of a serpent—spoke to Eve. Satan and Eve discussed God's instructions about the trees. Recall that God had commanded Adam simply not to eat from the tree of the knowledge of good and evil. Observe here, however, how Satan distorted God's Word and how Eve added to it:

> Now the serpent was more crafty than any of the
> wild animals the LORD God had made. He said to the
> woman, "Did God really say, 'You must not eat from *any*
> tree in the garden'?"
> The woman said to the serpent, "We may eat fruit
> from the trees in the garden,
> "but God did say, 'You must not eat fruit from the
> tree that is in the middle of the garden, *and you must not
> touch it,* or you will die.'"
>
> Genesis 3:1–3

Here, Eve amplified and distorted God's commandment to
Adam by stating that they could not even *touch* the tree of the
knowledge of good and evil.

Also, notice how the demonic spirit operated with Eve. He
was subtle. Using a friendly approach, he engaged Eve in
conversation, desiring to impress her. He lured her to exaggerate
God's command. We can see that a relationship and
communication started to develop between Eve and Satan.

Now, let's continue Eve's conversation with the devil:

> "You will *not* surely die," the serpent said to the
> woman.
> "For God knows that *when you eat of it your eyes will
> be opened....*"
>
> Genesis 3:4-5

Until this point, Eve did not know that her eyes had been
shut. She was curious about what the snake meant when he

said, "Your eyes will be opened." *Why would she desire to have her eyes opened? What would she see?*

Why could Satan allure Eve with this promise? Obviously this temptation attracted Eve to desire something more, but what was it?

Understand that the tree of the knowledge of good and evil did not contain fruit, as we normally would picture it. This was not an apple, pear, plum, peach, banana, or any other kind of tree with tangible, edible fruit. Remember, this was a tree of *knowledge.* Its fruit was knowledge. "Eating" from the tree of the knowledge of good and evil meant the ingestion of—or taking into oneself—an entirely different source of knowledge. That knowledge would cause the person to see good and evil and to decide right from wrong.

Now, Satan enticed Eve, stating that if she and Adam partook of the tree of the knowledge of good and evil, they would become like God:

> "For God knows that when you eat of it your eyes will be opened, and you will be like God, knowing good and evil."
>
> Genesis 3:5

Shortly, we will see that Satan accurately reported what this new source of information would do to Adam and Eve. His statement in verse five above is very similar to God's declaration later in this account (Genesis 3:22). If Adam and Eve were to eat from the tree of the knowledge of good and evil, they would ingest knowledge from a new spiritual source. That information would change their nature and cause them to see life differently. Unaware of the destruction that would follow, they would step into Satan's realm, knowing nothing of the chaos Satan had created in Genesis 1:1–2.

> In the beginning God created the heaven and the earth.
> And the earth was without form, and void; and darkness was upon the face of the deep. And the Spirit of God moved upon the face of the waters.
>
> Genesis 1:1-2 (KJV)

Understand that God does not create anything that is formless, empty, and ruled by darkness. Notice that in Genesis 1:2, above, the Holy Spirit *"moved* upon the face of the waters." The word *moved* means to brood over as a mother hen broods over her eggs until they hatch chickens. Likewise, the Holy Spirit knew the plan of God's creation. God Himself brought into existence exactly what He wanted:

1. The Holy Spirit, who was on the scene and knew God's plan, precisely moved into every area of destruction.

2. Then, when God called creation to be, the Holy Spirit's *brooding* and awesome power of God created the manifestation of His Words!

Remember, the Holy Spirit is a Liberator!

> Now the Lord is that Spirit: and where the Spirit of the Lord is, there is liberty.
>
> 2 Corinthians 3:17 (KJV)

Self-Deception Preceded Sin

In Genesis 3:6, before eating from the tree of the knowledge of good and evil, Eve had opened the doors of her heart and mind to deception:

> ...The woman *saw* that the fruit of the tree was *good for food* and *pleasing to the eye*, and also *desirable for gaining wisdom*....
>
> Genesis 3:6

Here, Eve started to become entangled with the world. The Bible warns:

> For all that is in the world, the lust of the flesh, and the lust of the eyes, and the pride of life, is not of the Father, but is of the world.
>
> 1 John 2:16 (KJV)

First, Eve looked at the fruit, which we must remember was knowledge. It appealed to her appetite for food (the lust of the flesh), was pleasant to behold (the lust of the eyes), and would make her wise (the pride of life). The Bible says that knowledge can make us prideful, especially if we do not love God.

> ...Knowledge puffs up, but love builds up.
> The man who thinks he knows something does not yet know as he ought to know.
> But the man who loves God is known by God.
>
> 1 Corinthians 8:1-3

Now, the devil tempted Eve in her area of vulnerability.

51

Demons do that. *Demon* is the Greek word *daimon* from the root *da,* which means "to know." Therefore, a *demon* is "a knowing one" or being.[1] The devil had watched Eve and knew how to communicate confusion, strife, division, and disobedience. However, she did have a choice. She could:

- Listen to Satan's enticing words.
- Or rebuke him.

Sadly, Eve chose to listen, and she assimilated the devil's evil into her own mind and heart. Then, she looked at that which God had forbidden. This is how the deceitfulness of sin works.

What happened next after Eve looked at the fruit on the tree of the knowledge of good and evil? Looking led to the committing of sin: Eating the forbidden fruit of another source of knowledge. Sin is deceitful. It lures people to act on the lies they grow to believe.

> ...She took some and ate it. She also gave some to her husband, who was with her, and he ate it.
>
> Genesis 3:6

This verse reveals that Adam was in proximity to Eve. Yet, he did not carry out his God-given role of protecting her from the enemy's voice. The man was in the environment of temptation and not only failed to stop it, but also partook. Both disobeyed and ate the forbidden fruit. In His mercy, however, God gave Adam and Eve time to repent. They did not.

The Effects of Ingesting New Knowledge

Suddenly, the effects of eating from the tree of the knowledge of good and evil became apparent:

Then the eyes of both of them were opened, and they realized they were naked; so they sewed fig leaves together and made coverings for themselves.

Then the man and his wife heard the sound of the LORD God as he was walking in the garden in the cool of the day, and they hid from the LORD God among the trees of the garden.

Genesis 3:7-8

Adam and Eve found refuge among the trees, but not from the tree of life. We will discuss in more detail why the tree of life was no longer accessible. However, they could not hide from God's presence.

But the LORD God called to the man, "Where are you?"

Genesis 3:9

Why didn't God call Eve? It is because He had delegated the authority and responsibility of obedience to Adam. Remember, God had instructed Adam—not Eve—about the trees in the garden. Therefore, God held him responsible for their adhering to the commandment. Not only was Adam responsible for himself, but also for his wife. He should have stopped the snake long before they ate the fruit!

He [Adam] answered, "I heard you in the garden, and I was *afraid*...."

Genesis 3:10

One of the first signs of eating from the tree of the knowledge of good and evil is fear. Fear is a product of man's Fall.

Adam's and Eve's Responses to their Sin

Let's continue Adam's conversation with God in verse ten:

> He [Adam] answered, "I heard you in the garden, and I was *afraid* because I was naked; so I hid."
> And he [God] said, "Who told you that you were naked? Have you eaten from the tree that I commanded you not to eat from?"
> The man said, *"The woman you put here with me—she gave me some fruit from the tree, and I ate it."*
>
> Genesis 3:10-12

In this passage, Adam accused God for giving the woman to him, accused the woman for giving the fruit to him, and excused himself. Adam did not take any responsibility for his sin. It is as if he had said, "I had my mouth open, and in it came! I could not stop what happened." Then, he put on a fig leaf, excused himself, and accused another.

> Then the LORD God said to the woman, "What is this you have done?" The woman said, "The serpent deceived me, and I ate."
>
> Genesis 3:13

Now, this is a true statement. When God confronted her, Eve did not try to hide her sin. She simply explained that Satan had tricked her and she had eaten.

Relationship is the problem here. You see, these deadly effects result from relating to the wrong spiritual source of information. It produces a curse.

The Curse

> So the LORD God said to the serpent, "Because you
> have done this, 'Cursed are you above all the livestock
> and all the wild animals! You will crawl on your belly
> and you will eat dust all the days of your life.'"
>
> Genesis 3:14

Because the devil had accessed the serpent's body, God
cursed the creature. Still speaking to the serpent, God continued:

> "And I will put enmity between you and the woman,
> and between your offspring and hers; he will crush your
> head, and you will strike his heel."
>
> Genesis 3:15

This is a prophetic statement about Jesus, the Messiah, who
would be born of God's Spirit unto a woman.
Then God continued:

> To the woman he said, "I will greatly increase your
> pains in childbearing; with pain you will give birth to
> children. Your desire will be for your husband, and he
> will rule over you."
>
> Genesis 3:16

Misinterpretation of this and the next verse has caused
major challenges within the Body of Christ, which we will
discuss later in this chapter.

> To Adam he said, "Because you listened to your wife

and ate from the tree about which I commanded you,
'You must not eat of it,' Cursed is the ground because of
you; through painful toil you will eat of it all the days of
your life."

Genesis 3:17

Do you realize that originally God did not design the ground
to be a dust bowl of frustration, pain, and suffering? It was to be
lush and fulfilling for man, animals, and plants—all of whom
would draw life from it and its rivers, streams, and aquifers.
However, because of the Fall, man would begin to toil in the
cultivation of the earth for food. The entirety of creation suffered
as a result of the curse!

It will produce thorns and thistles for you, and you
will eat the plants of the field.

Genesis 3:18

God had blessed Adam and Eve with a garden full of fruit
trees, which He had planted. Adam and Eve simply needed to
harvest their field.

Likewise, your heavenly Father is restoring back to you the
field that God planted for you! You *will* harvest! Your burden
shall be light, and your yoke is easy. Jesus said:

Take my yoke upon you, and learn of me; for I am
meek and lowly in heart: and ye shall find rest unto your
souls.

For my yoke is easy, and my burden is light.

Matthew 11:29-30 (KJV)

Now, let's continue our reading in Genesis about the curse:

"By the sweat of your brow you will eat your food until you return to the ground, since from it you were taken; for dust you are and to dust you will return."

Genesis 3:19

This means that no longer would man enjoy one of the areas God originally had planned for man's fulfillment. Yes, God designed man to enjoy the harvest. Now, to eat, he would have to work hard.

When a man does not derive fulfillment from his vocation, it becomes a curse, which drains him. When this happens, arguments about his work can erupt at home. This, then, can create within the wife a deep sense of insecurity, because she does not know where the next meal will come from. It may force her to leave home to go into the workforce.

I do not object to women working outside the home, by any means. However, the motivation behind her working is very, very critical. It should not be because the ground is so cursed for the man that she must come under that and share the curse with him. If this is the reason she works, she will not reap blessings for herself or her family. Then, her job will become a curse to her. This is not God's plan.

God's Plan to Reverse the Curse

Although man had fallen and had brought curse to the earth, God had a plan to redeem it all. Let's continue our reading in Genesis:

Adam named his wife Eve, because she would become the mother of all the living.

The LORD God made garments of skin for Adam and

57

his wife and clothed them.

Genesis 3:20–21

This is the first time physical death occurs in the Bible. Here, God killed an animal, or an angel could have done it. However, most likely God did, because the Bible says that God made the clothing.

Now, what was inside the coats of skins? It was blood. God covered Adam and Eve in blood. What does blood have to do with the curse? Well, it has everything to do with it! We find in Revelation 12:11:

> And they overcame him [Satan] by the blood of the Lamb [Jesus], and by the word of their testimony; and they loved not their lives unto the death.

Revelation 12:11 (KJV)

This verse foreshadows the spilling of Jesus' Blood in the final sacrifice for man's sin.

Adam and Eve had no idea what a sacrifice for sins was. Only recently had God created them and put them in the earth. Suddenly, (as we will read soon in Genesis) they could not reenter the garden and were not acclimated to living this new cursed life. As a result of the Fall, they suddenly knew only curse, and did not understand what had happened.

How Did this Fruit Affect Man?

Let's continue reading:

> And the LORD God said, "The man has now become like one of us, knowing good and evil."

Genesis 3:22a

Here is the confirmation of Satan's statement from Genesis 3:5, which we read earlier:

> "For God knows that when you eat of it [the tree of the knowledge of good and evil] your eyes will be opened, and you will be like God, knowing good and evil."
>
> Genesis 3:5

Then God declared about man:

> "He must not be allowed to reach out his hand and take also from the tree of life and eat, and live forever."
> So the LORD God banished him from the Garden of Eden to work the ground from which he had been taken.
> After he drove the man out, he placed on the east side of the Garden of Eden cherubim and a flaming sword flashing back and forth to guard the way to the tree of life.
>
> Genesis 3:22b–24

Before the Fall, Adam and Eve had eaten freely of the tree of life. However, afterward, God had to prevent them from eating from this tree ever again. Otherwise, they would live forever in their fallen state of knowing good and evil.

Doctrine of "Free Moral Agency of Man"

What does it mean, "to know good and evil"? The answer to this question is a very powerful revelation about man's ability to choose. Please read this section very carefully, since most people grossly misunderstand this topic. In fact, many Christians boast that man's power of choice is godly! This is a lie from your unseen enemy. We will discuss this in detail.

59

Have you heard people say, "Man is a free moral agent"? In other words, human beings are free to decide their own value system. Man can determine within himself whether something is good or not good for him. It is critical to understand that this mindset and decision path result from the tree of the knowledge of good and evil.

This shocking teaching has infiltrated Christian doctrines, and now many preachers teach that God created us this way. Some say it is our God-given right. In fact, if you study the underlying doctrines of Christian groups, you will discover that many contain the "free moral agency of man." However, "free will" in its extreme is secular humanism! In this teaching, man is at the center, not God and His Word.

The truth is that God did not make us this way. Adam's Fall gave us the choice between good and evil. Yes, each of us possesses the power of choice, but the origin of that choice is not God. *Choice* did not have its origin from communion with God. You see, before the Fall, Adam freely ate from the tree of life and walked in complete communion with God. Every part of his life—spirit, soul, and body—was in perfect union with each other and with God.

This means that he walked in absolute obedience to God. There was no struggle to obey, because Adam was filled only with perfect love for, faith in, and obedience to God and His good will. Sin had not yet entered the human race. Therefore, Adam did not struggle with choosing good or evil. All he knew was good. His eyes were not opened to good and evil. He simply lived a "good" lifestyle, because that is the result of perfect communion with God.

However, when Adam and Eve ate from the tree of the knowledge of good and evil, they fell. As a result, they broke their communion with God, and suddenly their eyes were opened to knowing both good and evil. Ingestion of this new information created a struggle within Adam and Eve that all mankind inherited: The choice between good and evil.

From this curse, a term called *will worship* resulted:

> Wherefore if ye be dead with Christ from the rudiments of the world, why, as though living in the world, are ye subject to ordinances,
>
> (Touch not; taste not; handle not;
>
> Which all are to perish with the using;) after the commandments and doctrines of men?
>
> Which things have indeed a show of wisdom in *will worship*, and humility, and neglecting of the body; not in any honour to the satisfying of the flesh.
>
> Colossians 2:20-23 (KJV)

Let's read this last verse in the *New International Version:*

> Such regulations [based on human commands and teachings] indeed have an appearance of wisdom, with their self-imposed worship, their false humility and their harsh treatment of the body, but they lack any value in restraining sensual indulgence.
>
> Colossians 2:23

In other words, after the Fall, man began to establish his own standards—even regarding how to worship God. Imagine man telling God how he would worship Him! No longer did man chart his course by God's Word and will, but by his own desires. In doing this, man put his will above God, making it an idol, an object of worship. Therefore, under the curse, man began to worship his own will to choose.

Which Tree Did Jesus Die On?

Jesus Christ came to restore man's communion with God. He came to set man free from the curse. Now we can freely walk in liberty, because Jesus "hung on a tree":

> Christ redeemed us from the curse of the law by becoming a curse for us, for it is written: "Cursed is everyone who is hung on a tree."
>
> Galatians 3:13

What tree did Jesus hang on? Did He hang on the tree of life? Did He hang on the tree of the knowledge of good and evil, or was it a fruit-bearing tree? Since Jesus became sin, this lends support to the thought that it was the tree of the knowledge of good and evil. There were many different means of capital punishment then: Stoning to death, beheading, and others. However, Jesus hung on a tree to die.

Recall that God barred Adam and Eve from the tree of life by assigning an angel as an impenetrable barrier. After they had eaten of the tree of the knowledge of good and evil, Adam and Eve had no access to the tree of life. God had to close that "door."

However, He had another plan to reopen the path to the tree of life. Jesus declared that He is the door:

> Then said Jesus unto them again, Verily, verily, I say unto you, I am the door of the sheep.
>
> John 10:7 (KJV)

> Jesus saith unto him, I am the way, the truth, and the

life: no man cometh unto the Father, but by me.

John 14:6 (KJV)

On that tree at Calvary, Jesus' death was the payment for sin. His death reversed the curse's power, which had come through Adam's eating from the tree of the knowledge of good and evil. Most believers have not discovered this yet. Many still see themselves bound by sin. However, Jesus became sin for us, and through death, He freed us to live!

Jesus Came to Restore Man's Right to Eat from the Tree of Life

Jesus Christ came to set man free from the curse. His death on the tree of the knowledge of good and evil liberated man to eat freely from the tree of life once again! Now, the Christian's spirit can partake again of the tree of life.

However, while we still exist on this earth, our souls and bodies are not yet fully redeemed. One day, we will go to Heaven with our souls and our born-again human spirits. Later, as Jesus is returning, our graves will open. Then, we will rise to possess immortal bodies like Jesus has. Remember, God calls us to experience only *full* liberty. In the meantime, we wash ourselves by continually reading God's Word to renew our souls, and we present our bodies to God as living sacrifices. In a later chapter, we will discuss this in further detail.

Therefore, I urge you, brothers, in view of God's mercy, to *offer your bodies as living sacrifices*, holy and pleasing to God—which is your spiritual [act of] worship.

Do not conform any longer to the pattern of this world, but *be transformed by the renewing of your mind.*

63

Then you will be able to test and approve what God's will is —
his good, pleasing and perfect will.

Romans 12:1-2

...Christ loved the church and gave himself up for her
to make her holy, cleansing her by *the washing with water through the word,*
and to present her to himself as a radiant church, without stain or wrinkle or any other blemish, but holy and blameless.

Ephesians 5:25-27

From Which Tree Do *You* Eat?

Because of Jesus' victory at Calvary, you can live, eat, and walk in the way of the tree of life instead of the tree of the knowledge of good and evil. However, after Adam's Fall, the door is also open for each of us to decide our own values, evaluating what is good and evil. If we set our own value system, this is the result of the tree of the knowledge of good and evil.

Have you ever heard the cliché, "Where are you coming from?" People often ask this when they cannot understand another's motive or perspective and have no common ground from which to communicate. For all of history, this has happened between the world and God's people. The cause of this conflict between believers and nonbelievers is very basic:

- Believers walk in the way of the tree of life.
- The world walks according to the tree of the knowledge of good and evil.

In other words, believers, through simple obedience, have a

biblical world-view, in which God solely requires obedience to His laws. On the other hand, nonbelievers cherish their secular-humanist world-view, in which man himself dictates right and wrong at his whims.

Therefore, when receiving information, you must ask, "Where are you coming from?" Is the source of this knowledge from God or the world—from the tree of life or the tree of the knowledge of good and evil?

With the insight you have read above, maybe the lack of revelation in this area has affected some of your basic Christian beliefs! If so, this can be greatly disconcerting, because it overthrows the core of your beliefs and creates major challenges. The solution is simple: Remove the fear of change in Jesus' Name. Embrace the reality that *you* are not the authority, but God and His Word are! Your part is to say, "YES!" to God's good and perfect will.

The tree of the knowledge of good and evil has influenced Christianity in a major way. Remember what a demon is. It is a *knowing* being, who empowers people with information to make their own decisions and be free moral agents. The final result of this lifestyle is spiritual death—eternal separation from God.

On the other hand, God calls His people to trust Him, submit to and obey His will, and live holy and blameless lives before Him. As Christians, we can eat freely from the tree of life, which produces the God-kind of life both on earth and in Heaven eternally.

Now, from which of these trees do *you* want to eat: The tree of life or the tree of the knowledge of good and evil? This is not only a question that determines where you will spend eternity, but also how you will live on earth.

Roles in Marriage as a Result of the Curse

Next, we will discuss an example of a dangerous doctrine that has infiltrated the Church in the area of marriage. Its roots come from the original curse in the Garden of Eden. If you have ingested this teaching, I urge you to repent and accept God's view of marriage. It can change your life, especially if you are married!

Recall the verses we studied earlier, in which God pronounced the curse on Adam and Eve after the Fall:

> To Adam he said, *"Because you listened to your wife* and ate from the tree about which I commanded you, 'You must not eat of it,' Cursed is the ground because of you; through painful toil you will eat of it all the days of your life."
>
> Genesis 3:17

Some men say of their wives, "I don't have to listen to this woman. She has nothing worthwhile to say. When a man listens to a woman, it causes trouble. The Bible even says to keep women silent in church." This is a distortion of God's Word, based upon an incorrect understanding of the context. When we take one verse out of context, we risk falling into error. To understand any doctrine, we must read all the Scriptures, not merely one verse. It is not godly to suppress women.

Well, what about the curse on Eve, which we read earlier?

> To the woman he [God] said, "I will greatly increase your pains in childbearing; with pain you will give birth to children. Your desire will be for your husband, and *he will rule over you."*
>
> Genesis 3:16

A major doctrine in the Church is that the man is the head of the household. In the true biblical sense, this is correct; but some have distorted this teaching to mean that the husband is like a dictator over his wife.

You must understand that in these verses of Genesis, God decreed the curse as the result of Adam's and Eve's sin. He explained the detriment, harm, pain, and suffering that men and women would walk in from that day forth. However, this was not God's original plan for Adam and Eve before the Fall.

Remember, God keeps His covenant with us, but this covenant operates with two sides. On one side is blessing, which results when we adhere to the covenant. On the other side is cursing, which comes when we breach our covenant with God.

> This day I call heaven and earth as witnesses against you that I have set before you life and death, blessings and curses. Now choose life, so that you and your children may live.
>
> Deuteronomy 30:19

Adam and Eve broke their covenant with God. Therefore, they and all future generations had to bear the consequences of that sin: The curse. However, Jesus removed that curse for us. We do not have to live under it any longer.

Let's examine another result of the misunderstanding in marriage. Envision a Bible-thumping man pounding his fist on a table, commanding, "Look, woman, you *will* submit to me, because the Bible says I have rule over you." Well, if such a couple wants to have a cursed marriage, which ends in destruction, this is one way to do it!

You see, it is a curse for a man to force his rule as a

taskmaster over his wife. As I mentioned, Jesus came to liberate us from the curse. The New Testament explains that the husband's position is not to dictate his commands to his wife. Jesus is her Lord as well as the husband's. Instead, the husband is to treat his wife as Jesus treats the Church. The Bible instructs:

> Submit to one another out of reverence for Christ.
> Wives, submit to your husbands as to the Lord.
> For the husband is the head of the wife as Christ is the head of the church, his body, of which he is the Savior.
> Now as the church submits to Christ, so also wives should submit to their husbands in everything.
> Husbands, love your wives, just as Christ loved the church and gave himself up for her
> to make her holy, cleansing her by the washing with water through the word,
> and to present her to himself as a radiant church, without stain or wrinkle or any other blemish, but holy and blameless.
> In this same way, husbands ought to love their wives as their own bodies. He who loves his wife loves himself.
> After all, no one ever hated his own body, but he feeds and cares for it, just as Christ does the church—
> for we are members of his body.
>
> Ephesians 5:21-30

You see, women can and do have the right of respect and mutual submission to God. A Christian man's wife is as much a joint-heir with Jesus as he is:

> The Spirit itself beareth witness with our spirit, that

we are the children of God:

And if children, then heirs; heirs of God, and joint-heirs with Christ; if so be that we suffer with him, that we may be also glorified together.

Romans 8:16-17 (KJV)

Likewise, ye husbands, dwell with them [your wives] according to knowledge, giving honour unto the wife, as unto the weaker vessel, and as being heirs together of the grace of life; that your prayers be not hindered.

Finally, be ye all of one mind, having compassion one of another, love as brethren, be pitiful, be courteous.

1 Peter 3:7-8 (KJV)

Yes, a man should be the head of his household and the leader of his family, but not in a tyrannical dictatorship. His leadership style should be like that of Jesus in His earthly ministry. Jesus was a servant who loved, nurtured, guided, trained, healed, and protected people. He was full of grace and mercy; showed gentleness, tenderness, and compassion; and was self-giving even to the point of literal self-sacrifice. Yet, when necessary, He rebuked and corrected people, but always with a motivation of love for the person and concern for the truth. This is the model for the Christian husband.

As we studied earlier, when Jesus came to the earth, He became cursed for us. He bore in His own body the penalty of Adam's and Eve's sin—and ours. Now, those who accept Jesus Christ as Lord and Savior are no longer bound by the curse. By His shed Blood, Jesus restored mankind (including women!) to the right relationship with God—as if sin had never happened—that Adam and Eve enjoyed before the Fall. Therefore, in Christ, men and women are equal before God, spiritually.

> For ye are all the children of God by faith in Christ
> Jesus.
> For as many of you as have been baptized into Christ
> have put on Christ.
> There is neither Jew nor Greek, there is neither bond
> nor free, there is neither male nor female: for ye are all
> one in Christ Jesus.
> And if ye be Christ's, then are ye Abraham's seed,
> and heirs according to the promise.
>
> Galatians 3:26-29 (KJV)

In Christian families, spouses first are equal brothers and sisters in Christ, then spouses second. We must treat our mates as fellow Christians, who have spiritual connections to God and therefore the Holy Spirit living inside them. The Christian wife's insight is a valuable tool to her husband. He should never dismiss it without ample consideration.

"Yes," you might say, "but what about the verses in the New Testament that say women should keep quiet in the church?" Let's read these passages:

> Women should remain silent in the churches. They
> are not allowed to speak, but must be in submission, as
> the Law says.
> If they want to inquire about something, they should
> ask their own husbands at home; for it is disgraceful for
> a woman to speak in the church.
>
> 1 Corinthians 14:34-35

A woman should learn in quietness and full submission.

I do not permit a woman to teach or to have authority over a man; she must be silent.

For Adam was formed first, then Eve.

1 Timothy 2:11-13

You see, Jesus liberated the family also. The curse in Genesis 3:16 many times is preached as God's order:

"...Your desire will be for your husband, and he will rule over you."

Genesis 3:16

However, this is not God's best for us. Instead, it is part of the curse that changed the relationship of husbands and wives and gave support to a slave-master relationship.

It would take an entire book to explain and thus eradicate the many distortions imposed upon families through religious traditions by man's wisdom, or the knowledge of good and evil.

In fact, this was Paul's goal in writing the above verses about women being silent in church. He simply was correcting women from shouting out their objections in church, asking them instead to share their spiritual concerns in their own homes. I do not think anyone would disagree with that simple correction. However, Paul never intended for it to become a doctrine of men as slave masters ruling their wives, as in many societies today around the world. This type of ruling is a curse, not God's blessing.

You see, whenever Scripture is distorted and brings bondage—"a life of restraint, hindrance, and ungodly limitation"—you must understand that the Holy Spirit is not communicating it this way. The Scripture plainly states in Romans 8:15:

> For *ye have not received the spirit of bondage* again to fear; but ye have received the Spirit of adoption, whereby we cry, Abba, Father.
>
> Romans 8:15 (KJV)

Additionally, the Word declares in 2 Corinthians 3:17:

> ...Where the Spirit of the Lord is, there is liberty.
>
> 2 Corinthians 3:17 (KJV)

Women are in the same Christ and have the same spiritual freedom as men.

For more information about relationships, marriage, and the biblical roles of husbands and wives, please contact our ministry. Available from our School of Victorious Living are materials such as:

- *What God Has Joined Together*
- *How to Fight for Your Family*
- *Relationships Your "Ruin or Rejoicing"*
- *The Power of the Lord's Blessing*
- *Dynamic Family*

These and other tools will help to train you in the Word of God regarding marriage and fulfillment in godly relationships.

Will You Obey God or Man?

How many of your thoughts (such as these above) can you

attribute not to God but to the tree of the knowledge of good and evil? How many cursed teachings have you heard? How many wrong beliefs have you adopted through family traditions, wrong leadership, and other means? You may need to tear down old mindsets, strongholds, fears, and false securities before God can restore His blessings to you.

> Casting down imaginations, and every high thing that exalteth itself against the knowledge of God, and bringing into captivity every thought to the obedience of Christ.
>
> 2 Corinthians 10:5 (KJV)

Today, I encourage you to put aside the fear of change. Then, cast down all ungodly things in your life—including evil thoughts, false doctrines, and fleshly habits—that do not originate from the knowledge of God and result in obedience to Christ. Dig up and pluck out the roots of the tree of the knowledge of good and evil in your life.

You see, God told Jeremiah that he had to uproot and destroy some things before he could build and plant:

> "See, today I appoint you over nations and kingdoms to uproot and tear down, to destroy and overthrow, to build and to plant."
>
> Jeremiah 1:10

We need to go through the same process in our lives. We must allow the washing of the water of the Word to give us a new mindset. This is especially key in eating from the tree of the knowledge of good and evil (which produces rebellion and results in curse) versus the tree of life (which produces obedience and therefore blessings).

If you want to develop in spiritual warfare, you cannot carry an attachment to the tree of the knowledge of good and evil. You see, to engage in spiritual warfare successfully, you must walk in the power and wisdom of the Holy Spirit of God. To do this, you must obey God, who sets the standards for right and wrong. If you eat from the tree of the knowledge of good and evil and set your own standards, you will walk in your own or Satan's power and wisdom, not in God's. This will result in spiritual defeat. You cannot conquer your unseen enemies in your own strength. Only God has the power for victory.

If you refuse to give up the tree of the knowledge of good and evil, you will continually evaluate your source of power and wisdom. *Is it the Holy Spirit,* you will ask yourself, *a demon, or me?* Because you have not sold out to God, it will be difficult for you to know the answer. Communion with God is the only way to be certain, and that only results from eating from the tree of life, not the tree of the knowledge of good and evil.

Turn away from the tree of the knowledge of good and evil. Do not say, for example, "There is nothing wrong with going to fortunetellers. They are just white witches. After all, they might be bad, but they're not all out of the same caldron." This kind of belief is man setting his own standard of good and evil. God declares in His Word:

> The acts of the sinful nature are obvious: sexual immorality, impurity and debauchery;
> idolatry and witchcraft; hatred, discord, jealousy,
> fits of rage, selfish ambition, dissensions, factions
> and envy; drunkenness, orgies, and the like. I warn

74

you, as I did before, that those who live like this will not inherit the kingdom of God.

Galatians 5:19-21

(See also Deuteronomy 18:9-13.) Instead of engaging in witchcraft or any of the above practices, these activities should set off alarms in your spirit.

Not only must you become knowledgeable of the truth, but also you must personally press in until the Holy Spirit transfers that knowledge into revelation. Otherwise, you will be open to deception.

In our Bible School courses, I teach that:

- Meditation brings revelation.
- Revelation brings motivation.
- Motivation brings action.
- Action brings the fruit.

You see, when you read the Bible or God reveals a portion of knowledge, you should meditate on it. To meditate on God's Word is to speak it over and over in your own hearing. Do this until it becomes more than merely information to you. It must become revelation. Revelation occurs when all obstacles are removed, and God's truth is uncovered and fully revealed. Only in communion with God can this happen. Then, you can effectively prevail over the enemy's lies, deceit, and attacks. Then, you participate jointly with God in His work:

For we are labourers together with God: ye are God's husbandry, ye are God's building.

1 Corinthians 3:9 (KJV)

Yes, God desires fellowship with and obedience from us. However, He does not want His children to obey Him blindly like puppets, fearing the consequences of disobedience. Instead, He desires for us to choose obedience *willingly,* yield to the Holy Spirit, and let Christ live through us. It is that simple. God said:

If you are *willing and obedient,* you will eat the best from the land.

Isaiah 1:19

Jesus said:

"Watch and pray so that you will not fall into temptation. The spirit is willing, but the body is weak."

Matthew 26:41

Turn the Curse into Blessing

Adam and Eve did not take any proactive steps to remove themselves from the influence of the enemy. They never asked for forgiveness. Additionally, they did not fully surrender their lives to Jehovah under His covenant of grace and blessing. Consequently, they paid a great price and fell from God's grace and blessing into cursing.

Jesus Christ turned all this around for you. Your life can be free of curses in Him. Be proactive. Remember, knowledge puffs up but love builds up. Love yourself enough to spend time with your Father God to seek Him. Become intimate in your relationship with Jesus. Ask for the Holy Spirit to fill you and give to you the Knowing Gifts: the Word of Knowledge, the Word of Wisdom, and the Discerning of Spirits. (See 1 Corinthians 12:7-11.) You can and will see beyond the apparent.

Even if no one else in your family receives God's revelation knowledge, you can be the one who does, thereby sanctifying your home:

> For the unbelieving husband is sanctified by the wife, and the unbelieving wife is sanctified by the husband: else were your children unclean; but now are they holy.
>
> 1 Corinthians 7:14 (KJV)

Remember to:

1. Wash your mind and thinking by constant Bible study.

2. Identify every source of ungodly information, locate its area of involvement in your life, and eradicate it in Jesus' Name.

3. Take back your life in Christ and penetrate every realm of darkness until you prevail over your unseen enemies.

8
Conquer Your Sin Nature through Christ

Too many Christians live defeated lives simply because they do not understand that Jesus completely defeated the sin nature. They do not realize that when they accepted Christ as Lord and Savior, they became righteous in Him. Grasping this revelation knowledge is the believer's first step to defeating the unseen enemies.

In this chapter, we will discuss how Jesus defeated your sin nature, so you can understand God's plan for your new life.

God Had a Plan

Before Adam and Eve disobeyed Him, God had a plan for man's redemption, as we discussed in the previous chapter. When they partook of the fruit of the tree of the knowledge of good and evil, their natures changed. By committing the act that God had prohibited, the very nature of Satan entered into them. That sin nature took over and ruled Adam, his wife, and *all* of their descendants—the entire human race. This is what Paul meant when he wrote:

> Wherefore, as by one man sin entered into the world, and death by sin; and so death passed upon all men, for that all have sinned.
>
> Romans 5:12 (KJV)

What does this mean? The sin nature passed from one human to another through all generations.

Adam brought death to many, but Jesus Christ brings life!

> But the gift is not like the trespass. For if the many died by the trespass of the one man, how much more did God's grace and the gift that came by the grace of the one man, Jesus Christ, overflow to the many!
>
> Romans 5:15

God's original plan was to create humanity to be in permanent fellowship with Himself. However, Satan deceived Eve, Adam fell with her, and they both partook of the satanic nature. Yet, God had a plan of redemption. He sent Jesus to remove from man the spiritual sin nature, which held him captive. This was the purpose of Jesus Christ's coming to the earth—to destroy the sin nature in mankind and all the works of the devil, as we will discuss next.

Jesus Defeated the Sin Nature

A major misconception exists among many Christian believers. The misunderstanding is this: After becoming born again, Christians have two natures in their hearts or spirits. Many wrongly believe that we have a sin nature, from which we never can become completely free; and the nature of God, in which we never are worthy to walk. Guilt, shame, condemnation, inferiority, and insecurity hold down many Christians because of this belief. The truth is now the nature of sin can influence only your body.

It is critical that you receive this revelation: God has given absolute victory to you over the sin nature. If you miss this, your triumph in life becomes a fleeting hope. When you try to battle your unseen enemy on *his* ground—the sin nature—he defeats you before you begin.

You see, if you are a Christian, the Spirit of God is in you:

> You, however, are controlled not by the sinful nature but by the Spirit, if the Spirit of God lives in you....
>
> Romans 8:9a

Now, when you battle the enemy, it is not your old sin nature but the Spirit of God who fights—and wins every time! You are in Christ. When Jesus died, you died in Him. Your sin nature died in His death. Then, when He rose from the dead, you rose in Him. The Holy Spirit now lives in you.

> If *ye then be risen with Christ,* seek those things which are above, where *Christ sitteth on the right hand of God.*
>
> Set your affection on things above, not on things on the earth.
>
> For *ye are dead, and your life is hid with Christ* in God.
>
> When Christ, who is our life, shall appear, then shall ye also appear with him in glory.
>
> Colossians 3:1-4 (KJV)

As you can see in the above passage, you have the authority, through Jesus' death, to say to sin, "I am dead and my life is hid with Christ." Quote aloud the verse below:

> I am crucified with Christ: nevertheless I live; yet not I, but Christ liveth in me: and the life which I now live in the flesh I live by the faith of the Son of God, who loved

me, and gave himself for me.

Galatians 2:20 (KJV)

So, now, take action. Read and obey Romans 6:1-12.

Likewise reckon ye also yourselves to be dead indeed unto sin, but alive unto God through Jesus Christ our Lord.

Let not sin therefore reign in your mortal body, that ye should obey it in the lusts thereof.

Romans 6:11-12 (KJV)

If you are a Christian, you have authority over the power of sin, through Jesus. That's why Jesus came to earth:

...For the devil sinneth from the beginning. For this purpose the Son of God was manifested, that he might destroy the works of the devil.

1 John 3:8 (KJV)

Jesus came to "destroy the works of the devil." Well, the first work of the devil was *sin.* When we understand this, we can see more clearly the benefits of Jesus Christ's redemptive work. Therefore, when we engage in spiritual warfare, we should not feel unworthy, unfit, or unable to have dominion and authority over our unseen enemies. Jesus wrought our victory over Satan by the same power of the Holy Spirit who now dwells in us!

Sin Versus Sins

Every person who is not born again is a spiritual child of Satan. In the first part of the above verse we just read, John wrote:

82

He that *committeth sin* is of the devil; for the devil
sinneth from the beginning.

1 John 3:8a (KJV)

The phrase *committeth sin* literally means "continues in the
practice of sinning" or "is habitually bound to sinning."

Sin is the nature of Satan. He is the first sinner, and he sinned
from the beginning. Satan was the first being to experience a
nature change, as we will study later:

Thou art the anointed cherub that covereth; and I
have set thee so: thou wast upon the holy mountain of
God; thou hast walked up and down in the midst of the
stones of fire.

Thou wast perfect in thy ways from the day that thou
wast created, till iniquity was found in thee.

Ezekiel 28:14-15 (KJV)

The word *sin*, in the singular, means the *nature of sin*, not *acts
of sinning*. The motivation that drives an unbeliever to sin
habitually is the nature of sin. The sin nature is the spiritual
proclivity inside an unbeliever to fall short of God's standards.
It is not sins, but sin—not wrong actions, but a wrong nature—
that separates an unbeliever from God.

This is why religion that tries to bring a person into fellowship
with God through good works is doomed to fail. Man's good
works can never remove the sin nature. Only Jesus did this.

On the other hand, something creative occurs in a person's
life when he is born-again. The part of us that becomes born-
again is our re-created human spirits. When this happens, we
no longer have two natures in our spirits.

No one who is born of God will *continue to sin*, because God's seed remains in him; he cannot go on sinning, because he has been born of God.

1 John 3:9

Notice, this does *not* say we are unable to commit *sins*. This verse means that we do not commit sin *through the nature of sin*. The sin nature is no longer present within us. When we were born-again, the sin nature was broken and removed from us.

Now, every Christian believer can commit *sins*. I am not suggesting that when you become born-again, it is impossible for you ever to commit a wrong act. All of us have acted or thought wrongly and then asked the Lord to forgive us.

However, what causes a believer and an unbeliever to sin are two entirely different concepts. If we do not understand the difference, we mistakenly will think that the sin nature burdens us with sin from which we can never become free. That is not true.

If you are a Christian, and you find yourself sinning, it is *not* because you have the sin nature within you and will be bound to it for the rest of your life. No! You have the nature of God Himself within you. When you sin, quickly repent with the intention of never committing that sin again. Get back up, dust yourself off, and *know* that the Holy Spirit is in you to empower you to live a holy life. You see, you *can* live a holy life, set apart for God, and not carry the constant burden of sin. Later, we will discuss this in another chapter.

The forgiveness of sins did not redeem us. What redeemed us was the removal of our sin nature. As believers, we still need forgiveness for the sins we commit. On the other hand, unbelievers need something more drastic. They need the *nature* of sin removed. As we studied earlier, this is God's purpose for sending Jesus to the earth.

Jesus—the Man—Defeated Satan

When reading the story of Satan's original rebellion against God, people often ask an important question. If Satan caused God so much trouble, why didn't God simply zap him? The more we understand the Bible, the more we realize why a God of justice would not do this. Certainly God *could* have dethroned the enemy through an outright display of power. However, as we shall see, it is more fitting that God chose to become a man to defeat the devil.

When God created the earth, He delegated to man the authority to run this planet. However, as we studied earlier, the first man, Adam, sold his control of the earth to Satan. Now, the most fitting way to take back that authority from Satan was for a man to seize it. God wanted a man to take back what man had given away. So God became man in the Person of Jesus. As a man, Jesus defeated the enemy on the same plane in which Satan had defeated man. Jesus beat our unseen enemy on Satan's home field.

Think about it for a moment. If a ball player wanted to win every game, he could do it by shooting all his opponents with a machine gun. When each team did not show up, he would win *every* game. However, would that be just or godly? Of course it would not. To win legitimately, the ball player must play by the rules.

In the same way, God—seated on His throne in Heaven—has the power to win every game. He could have overthrown Satan simply by zapping him. Instead, He chose to come as a man to defeat Satan on the same terms by which Satan had defeated man. God would not think of dethroning the enemy any other way.

The letter to the Hebrews tells us Jesus was tempted and suffered everything all men ever would endure. Why? To overcome legally, Jesus had to be on the same plane as all human beings—tempted, tried, persecuted, afflicted, and abandoned—as we are. He would live and die here as a man.

> Since the children have flesh and blood, he too shared in their humanity so that by his death he might destroy him who holds the power of death—that is, the devil—
>
> and free those who all their lives were held in slavery by their fear of death.
>
> For surely it is not angels he helps, but Abraham's descendants.
>
> For this reason he had to be made like his brothers in every way, in order that he might become a merciful and faithful high priest in service to God, and that he might make atonement for the sins of the people.
>
> Because he himself suffered when he was tempted, he is able to help those who are being tempted.
>
> Hebrews 2:14-18

Jesus' victory over Satan is awesome. He defeated Satan through His humanity as the "Son of Man," not the "Son of God."

Remember, in Genesis, God said to the serpent—that is, to Satan:

> And I will put enmity between thee and the woman, and between thy seed and her seed; it shall bruise thy head, and thou shalt bruise his heel.
>
> Genesis 3:15 (KJV)

This was a prophecy that God spoke concerning Jesus Christ, the coming "seed" of the woman. This would be the man to defeat Satan as we read in 1 John 3:8.

Satan has tricked Christians into thinking: *Since Jesus was God on earth, He could do anything.* This is why many become very confused about Satan's dethroning. They do not see the fullness of victory that Jesus gave to man through His humanity. If Jesus had defeated Satan purely as God, we would be grateful, of course. However, because He—as a man—defeated Satan, we actually can join in Jesus' victory! Now, we, too, have victory over Satan—our unseen enemy!

Two Adams

The Bible discusses two Adams who have lived on the earth:

> So it is written: "The first man Adam became a living being"; the last Adam, a life-giving spirit.
>
> 1 Corinthians 15:45

Who was the first Adam? He was the one in the garden, the one who ate the fruit. Who was the last Adam? Jesus fits this description: "A life-giving spirit."

> The first man was of the dust of the earth, the second man from heaven.
> As was the earthly man, so are those who are of the earth; and as is the man from heaven, so also are those who are of heaven.
> And just as we have borne the likeness of the earthly man, so shall we bear the likeness of the man from heaven.
>
> 1 Corinthians 15:47-49

Each of us is the offspring of either the first or second Adam. If we are born of the first Adam (who lived in the garden), his sin nature separates us from fellowship with God. On the other hand, if we are born-again of the second Adam (Jesus), we are spiritual children of God, and the sin nature is no longer in us.

We Are Alive with Christ

Paul explained how this works:

> As for you, *you were dead in your transgressions and sins,*
> in which you used to live when you followed the ways of this world and of the ruler of the kingdom of the air, the spirit who is now at work in those who are disobedient.
> All of us also lived among them at one time, gratifying the cravings of our sinful nature and following its desires and thoughts. Like the rest, we were by nature objects of wrath.
> But because of his great love for us, God, who is rich in mercy,
> *made us alive with Christ even when we were dead in transgressions* — it is by grace you have been saved.
> For we are God's workmanship, created in Christ Jesus to do good works, which God prepared in advance for us to do.
>
> Ephesians 2:1-5, 10

Paul wrote these lines to a Church that is not dead anymore. Once we were dead. Once we were separated, mired in trespasses and sins. However, Jesus came to bring life to those who were dead—to remove the sin nature that leads to separation from God.

88

Jesus Willingly Took on Satan's Sin Nature

Jesus Christ died so the sin nature no longer would control God's creation.

> Yet it pleased the LORD to bruise him [Jesus]; he hath put him to grief: when thou shalt make his soul an offering for sin....
>
> Isaiah 53:10 (KJV)

God made Jesus "an offering for sin." Through His Son, God poured out His wrath upon mankind, not because of what we did but because of whose we were. We were children of the devil. The same wrath that God had poured on Satan also fell upon mankind and specifically upon Jesus at Calvary.

Jesus' soul became sin. It was not because He *wanted* a sin nature, but because He *had to have* a sin nature. God needed a substitute upon whom He could pour all His wrath. Man had to have a substitute to suffer the wrath for him. Jesus Christ became sin for us, so we could become righteous in Him.

> For he [God] hath made him [Jesus] to be sin for us, who knew no sin; that we might be made the righteousness of God in him.
>
> 2 Corinthians 5:21 (KJV)

Many Christians limit themselves because they do not understand the full extent of what Jesus has done for them. He did not merely use His cosmic eraser to eradicate our particular acts of sin. No, the Son of God allowed Himself to become a man and His soul to become the spiritual nature of Satan.

No man killed Jesus. He declared:

89

...I lay down my life....

John 10:17 (KJV)

He willingly took upon Himself the sin nature. Before the foundations of the earth, Jesus knew that He would do this. Jesus' death on the cross was not a surprise that God sprang on Him in the garden of Gethsemane. Jesus knew His purpose was to go to the cross. This was the goal of His coming to earth, to bear the nature that formerly controlled your life and mine. He knew that He would receive Satan's nature on the cross. This is how Jesus was to loose mankind from the shackles of the sin nature and conquer our unseen enemies.

You Are Righteous in Christ

In conclusion, remember, you are a new person in Christ.

Likewise reckon ye also yourselves to be dead indeed unto sin, but alive unto God through Jesus Christ our Lord.

Romans 6:11 (KJV)

If you have accepted Jesus Christ as your Lord and Savior, then realize that you are no longer a sinner. Sin has no dominion or control over you anymore. You are a new creation, because Jesus removed the sin nature from you. Reckon fully that you are not a sinner any longer. You need not walk in guilt and condemnation again.

Because Jesus Christ died to remove your sin nature, no longer are you under the subjection of any kind of sin. The reason the Son of God died was to remove from your life that controlling entity called the sin nature. Now you reign triumphantly with Him in righteousness. *Righteousness* means that you stand in the presence of God without inferiority or guilt, as though sin or the sin nature had never existed in you.

You must see this about yourself. When you were born again, Jesus removed the sin nature from you. No longer do the world, the lust of the flesh, the lust of the eyes, and the pride of life have dominion over you. Your freedom does not rest on how strong *you* are, but on the death of Jesus Christ. He placed you into a position called righteousness. Jesus has conquered your unseen enemies. Now, you must learn how to walk in this powerful victory.

9
Walk in Your New-Creation Life

New Testament Christianity is a triumphant life of God's power and dominion in the believer's life. The Church is not to be a weak, sick, and beggarly bunch. No, as believers we should walk in the resurrected life of Jesus in absolute triumph and victory!

The problem is that man's "wisdom" and doctrines of the enemy have deceived many in the Church, today. Jesus said:

> *Making the word of God of none effect through your tradition,* which ye have delivered: and many such like things do ye.
> Mark 7:13 (KJV)

I did not say this. Jesus did! Here, we see that man's wisdom and doctrines of traditional teaching literally nullify the power of the Word of God. Consequently, the Church is not a triumphant, victorious, and overcoming group of believers who successfully defeat the devil's works. Instead, the Body of Christ has been trying to figure out what is wrong.

In this chapter, we will discuss who we are as Christians, what our position is in Christ, and how to get back on the track of victory.

New Creatures, Like Jesus

Jesus rose from the dead to be a new-creation man on the face of the earth. Later in this chapter, we will see that God intended for this new man, Jesus Christ, to be a twin with every man and woman on earth. We are to be His brothers and sisters.

It is critical to understand that our new-life victory does not rest upon ourselves. It does not rest upon how strong or determined we are, or on how much we pray or read the Bible. Our triumph rests upon Jesus—what He did for us when He rose from the dead. This is the foundation of our victory. Remember, we died and rose when Jesus did (Colossians 3:1-4). His triumph is our triumph. God re-created us in Him. This is why the Bible says that those who are in Christ are new creatures:

> Therefore, if anyone is in Christ, he is a new creation; the old has gone, the new has come!
>
> 2 Corinthians 5:17

What are these new creatures like? We are like Jesus!

> For those God foreknew he also predestined to be *conformed to the likeness of his Son,* that he might be *the firstborn among many brothers.*
>
> Romans 8:29

There is no difference between us. You and I are one, and we are one with Jesus! We are brothers and sisters not only with fellow Christians, but also with Christ Himself!

Jesus became what you and I were, so we might become what He is! When you accept Him as your Lord and Savior, you become a new creation in Christ. Now, you can conquer your unseen enemy—the devil—because Jesus did.

We Are the Church of the Firstborn

Notice that Romans 8:29, which we read above, states that Jesus "might be the firstborn among many brothers." He led the way for you and me, His brothers and sisters. Now, we have a forerunner in Heaven, a man—yes, a man like us. He paved the way for us to follow Him to Heaven.

Not only was Jesus "the firstborn among many brothers," but the Bible also says that He was "the firstborn of every creature" and "the firstborn from the dead":

> [Jesus] Who is the image of the invisible God, *the firstborn of every creature:*
>
> For by him were all things created, that are in heaven, and that are in earth, visible and invisible, whether they be thrones, or dominions, or principalities, or powers: all things were created by him, and for him:
>
> And he is before all things, and by him all things consist.
>
> And he is the head of the body, the church: who is the beginning, *the firstborn from the dead;* that in all things he might have the preeminence.
>
> Colossians 1:15-18 (KJV)

What does *firstborn from the dead* mean? Although it was uncommon, there were cases of people who had come back from the dead before Jesus died and rose. For example, remember Lazarus? When Jesus commanded, "Lazarus, come forth," the man came back to life. (See John 11:1-45.) Jairus' daughter also came back from the dead when Jesus healed her. (See Mark 5:21-43.)

However, Jesus did not merely *come back* from the dead. He was *born* from the dead. There is a difference. Lazarus and Jairus' daughter died again. This is not true of Jesus. He was born from the dead, never to die again.

Jesus was the first to die and then live again eternally. This is how He paved the way for us to go to Heaven. In the resurrection of Jesus Christ, God simply did not bring a man back from death, who ultimately died again and remains buried. No, He brought forth Jesus as the first new-creation man with a glorified body. Jesus yet reigns both in Heaven and on earth and has total dominion over all the works of the enemy!

When Jesus Christ became "the firstborn from the dead," every new-creation man and woman received the same spiritual nature of Jesus. Christians began to walk in the same triumph, dominion, authority, and provision that Jesus had in His life. This is why the writer of Hebrews called the Body of Christ "the church of the firstborn" in Hebrews 12:23.

The Bible teaches us that as Jesus is, "so are we in this world":

> Herein is our love made perfect, that we may have boldness in the day of judgment: because *as he is, so are we in this world.*
>
> 1 John 4:17 (KJV)

The Word of God does not say, "As He is, so are we *trying* to become." Many people try to become like Jesus, but cannot. No, either we *are* or *are not* like Him. If we are Christians, then we *are* like Him! We are the children of God—brothers and sisters of Jesus the Firstborn. Anything that says otherwise is a lie from the devil!

We Sit in God's Heavenly Realms with Jesus

Today, Jesus sits at the right hand of God:

> The eyes of your understanding being enlightened; that ye may know what is the hope of his calling, and

what the riches of the glory of his inheritance in the saints,

And what is the exceeding greatness of his power to us-ward who believe, according to the working of his mighty power,

Which he wrought in Christ, when he raised him from the dead, and *set him at his own right hand in the heavenly places,*

Far above all principality, and power, and might, and dominion, and every name that is named, not only in this world, but also in that which is to come:

And hath *put all things under his feet,* and gave him to be the head over all things to the church,

Which is his body, the fulness of him that filleth all in all.

Ephesians 1:18-23 (KJV)

God made Jesus the Head of the Body of Christ. No one can separate Him from the Church. That would be separating the Head of the Church from the Body of the Church. We are one with Jesus, and we function together as a unit.

Ephesians continues, saying that we now sit with Jesus in the heavenly realm:

And God raised us up with Christ and seated us with him in the heavenly realms in Christ Jesus.

Ephesians 2:6

We studied earlier that when Jesus rose again from the dead, we rose together with Him. Here, in Ephesians 2:6, we see that we rose to sit with Him in heavenly places. Now, we have the same position, authority, and dominion of Jesus Himself.

[Jesus Christ] Who is gone into heaven, and is on the right hand of God; angels and authorities and powers being made subject unto him.

1 Peter 3:22 (KJV)

"Angels and authorities and powers" are subject to us, now. How can that be? Our Big Brother, Jesus, is sitting together with us at the right hand of God the Father; and everything that is subject to Him is subject to us. Today, every demon in all creation is subject to you, if you are a Christian. We know this, because God's Word says it is true. We simply need to start *acting* as though it were true. The Apostle Paul encouraged us:

The weapons we fight with are not the weapons of the world. On the contrary, they have divine power to demolish strongholds.

2 Corinthians 10:4

Where does our power for spiritual warfare come from? Remember, it does not come from ourselves. This is why so many people have a hard time with deliverance. They think they have to battle the devil. Well, I have good news. We do, but not on our own. Remember, Paul wrote:

Finally, be strong in the Lord and in his mighty power.

Ephesians 6:10

How can we do this? We do it by simply believing: "I am strong in the Lord and in His mighty power." I live every day that way. I no longer know how to be weak.

Paul also wrote:

Nay, in all these things we are more than conquerors through him that loved us.

Romans 8:37 (KJV)

We are not "more than conquerors" through our physical, mental, or emotional abilities. No, we are more than conquerors through Jesus.

Jesus Is Our Brother

As we have read, Jesus Christ is the Firstborn:

- From the dead (Colossians 1:18).
- Of every creature (Colossians 1:15).
- Among many brothers (Romans 8:29).

He actually became the forerunner of absolute triumph over death, so we could live a new-creation life. Now, we are His brothers in triumph.

You and I come from the same source as Jesus. My earthly brother and I come from our earthly father. Likewise, Jesus and I have that very same relationship with God our Heavenly Father. So do you, if you are a Christian. That is why Jesus is not ashamed to call us His brothers.

> Both the one who makes men holy and those who are made holy *are of the same family. So Jesus is not ashamed to call them brothers.*
>
> Hebrews 2:11

Now, do you see more clearly why two different natures do not exist within a Christian's spirit: The sin nature and the divine nature? No, there is only one: The divine nature of Jesus Christ—the new-creation life. All Christians have it! Remember, our sin natures died on the cross with Jesus. Now, we live only in the new-creation nature.

Jesus Lives to Intercede for Us

Now, we have learned that Jesus:

- Is the Firstborn from the dead, among brothers, and of all creation (Romans 8:29, Colossians 1:15-18).
- Reigns from Heaven at the right hand of God over the enemy (Ephesians 1:18-23).

The story does not end there. Next, we will see that Jesus:

- Lives forever to intercede for us (Romans 8:34, Hebrews 7:25).

Now in Heaven, our Lord and Savior does not leave us to carry out the Kingdom's work alone.

> ...It is Christ that died, yea rather, that is risen again, who is even *at the right hand of God, who also maketh intercession for us.*
>
> Romans 8:34 (KJV)

> Wherefore he [Jesus] is able also to save them to the uttermost that come unto God by him, seeing he *ever liveth to make intercession for them.*
>
> Hebrews 7:25 (KJV)

We can rest, knowing that Jesus is watching over us and interceding continually on our behalf. What more do we need to conquer our unseen enemies and live in victory?

Jesus' Resurrection Purchased a New Creation

Jesus rose again from the dead by the power of the Holy Spirit. When you and I became born-again, it was also by the Holy Spirit. We became new creations and experienced God's power and presence. However, this did not happen in 1950, 1960, 1970, 1980, 1990, or whenever we accepted Christ into our lives. Remember, when Jesus became the Firstborn from the dead, so did we. Therefore, we were born-again two thousand years ago, when Jesus rose from the dead and became the first new-creation man!

When you accepted Christ, you simply accepted His finished work for you. One day you said, "I believe in my heart that God raised Jesus from the dead." No matter how it happened or where you were when you said this, your *confession* (of Jesus' resurrection and Jesus as Lord of your life) brought salvation. How can this be? The book of Romans says:

> That if thou shalt *confess with thy mouth* the Lord Jesus, and shalt *believe in thine heart that God hath raised him from the dead,* thou shalt be saved.
> For with the heart man believeth unto righteousness; and with the mouth confession is made unto salvation.
> Romans 10:9-10 (KJV)

What must you believe about the resurrection, as required according to verse nine, here? Believe that when Jesus rose again from the dead, He became the Head of a new creation. Also, you must believe that you became a new creation in Christ the moment you became a Christian.

Praise be to the God and Father of our Lord Jesus Christ! In his great mercy he has given us new birth into a living hope through the resurrection of Jesus Christ from the dead.

1 Peter 1:3

Now, all that remains is for you to walk in the truth of your finished victory in Christ.

10
Master Your Thoughts and Words

It is vital that you learn to master your thoughts and words. However, before you can do this, you first must discover the source of your thoughts. Only then will you know whether to reject or embrace the "wisdom" that comes your way. This chapter will help you to understand what causes your thoughts.

Four Sources of Wisdom

The following passages of Scripture reveal several sources of wisdom.

> We do, however, speak a message of wisdom among the mature, but not *the wisdom of this age or of the rulers of this age,* who are coming to nothing.
>
> No, we speak of *God's secret wisdom,* a wisdom that has been hidden and that God destined for our glory before time began.
>
> None of the rulers of this age understood it, for if they had, they would not have crucified the Lord of glory.
>
> However, as it is written:
>> "No eye has seen,
>>   no ear has heard,
>> no mind has conceived
>>   what God has prepared for those who love him"—
> but God has revealed it to us by His Spirit.

The Spirit searches all things, even the deep things of God.

For who among men knows the thoughts of a man except the man's spirit within him? In the same way no one knows the thoughts of God except the Spirit of God.

We have not received the spirit of the world but the Spirit who is from God, that we may understand what God has freely given us.

This is what we speak, not in words taught us by *human wisdom* but in words taught by the Spirit, expressing spiritual truths in spiritual words.

1 Corinthians 2:6-13

But if ye have bitter envying and strife in your hearts, glory not, and lie not against the truth.

This wisdom descendeth not from above, but is *earthly, sensual, devilish.*

James 3:14-15 (KJV)

Let's examine the three sources of "wisdom" that are not from God. I will call these: Human reason, flesh, and Satan. Lastly, we will discuss the fourth source of wisdom: the Holy Spirit.

Human reason. The first source of "wisdom" James mentions is "earthly." This is our natural human reason or logic. For example, when you want to drive a car, this is what tells you to get the key first. Your mind continually operates as a reasoning faculty.

These thoughts originate in carnal reasoning. Let's look at another example. It seems "reasonable" to become angry with someone because of a wrongdoing. However, James warned that if we stay on this earthly plane, we will become unforgiving, bitter, resentful, and selfish.

There is nothing wrong with reason as long as it does not exalt itself against the knowledge of God. As we studied in a previous chapter, the Bible explains what to do with anything that does this:

> We demolish arguments and every pretension that sets itself up against the knowledge of God, and we take captive every thought to make it obedient to Christ.
>
> 2 Corinthians 10:5

If our human reasoning has a thought that is contrary to the Word of God, we are to "demolish" it! For example, reason says, "I can do only what I am strong enough to do." On the other hand, the Bible says:

> I can do all things through Christ which strengtheneth me.
>
> Philippians 4:13 (KJV)

There is a big difference, here! We need to think as God's Word tells us.

Reason says, " I have only so much education. Therefore, I can earn only so much money." However, the Bible says:

> But my God shall supply all your need according to his riches in glory by Christ Jesus.
>
> Philippians 4:19 (KJV)

The Bible does not say that your education limits you. No, it is your obedience to the Word of God:

> Only be thou strong and very courageous, that thou

mayest observe to do according to all the law, which Moses my servant commanded thee: turn not from it to the right hand or to the left, that thou mayest prosper whithersoever thou goest.

This book of the law shall not depart out of thy mouth; but thou shalt meditate therein day and night, that thou mayest observe to do according to all that is written therein: for then thou shalt make thy way prosperous, and then thou shalt have good success.

Have not I commanded thee? Be strong and of a good courage; be not afraid, neither be thou dismayed: for the LORD thy God is with thee whithersoever thou goest.

Joshua 1:7-9 (KJV)

Here, the Bible promises that you will be prosperous and successful if you obey God. If your reasoning tells you otherwise, your mind is lying to you! Demolish that thought.

Flesh. The second kind of "wisdom" James described as "sensual." This is our flesh, which speaks to our minds through "the lust of the flesh, and the lust of the eyes, and the pride of life," as we studied earlier:

For all that is in the world, the lust of the flesh, and the lust of the eyes, and the pride of life, is not of the Father, but is of the world.

1 John 2:16 (KJV)

Like Eve, today many Christians allow the lust of the flesh, the lust of the eyes, and the pride of life to lead them. They walk about like unbelievers.

Have you ever had a lustful thought? That was your flesh

speaking. Your body was sending communications about its inordinate affection for something.

Have your eyes suddenly glanced somewhere even as you thought, *I don't want to look at that?* You may think this is a normal, involuntary action, but actually it is not. These kinds of urges are subject to your control. However, until you identify the source of this communication with your mind, your eyes will be everywhere.

Satan and/or Demons. The third source of "wisdom" James discussed is the voice of the evil one. This is "devilish." The Greek word for *devilish* means "resembling or proceeding from an evil spirit, demon-like"[1] or demonic in nature. We can receive "wisdom" directly from demons. As we saw with Eve, Satan can speak to our minds. Strongholds and "high things" come from the enemy, who communicates to us through our minds. He speaks deception, confusion and lust.

Holy Spirit. The fourth main source of wisdom is the Holy Spirit. The Bible explains how to recognize this wisdom from above:

> But the wisdom that comes from heaven is first of all pure; then peace loving, considerate, submissive, full of mercy and good fruit, impartial and sincere.
>
> James 3:17

Select Your Source of Wisdom

Only when you know its source, can you handle every thought that comes to you with confidence and ease. Picture it this way: You have a spiritual antenna on top of your head. The beams from channels 3, 6, 10, and 12—the four sources of wisdom—always bombard that antenna. Constantly, your mind receives the voice of the enemy, the voice of human reason, the voice of the flesh, and the voice of God through your human spirit. Realize that you have within you a spiritual channel selector. You can choose which voice you want to listen to. Now, which will you select?

Recognize the Source of Your Thoughts

Let's say that you are driving over a bridge, and this thought comes to your mind: *Drive off the bridge!* That surely is not human reason. It is not the lust of the flesh, because your flesh surely does not want to go into the water. It is not God, because He does not want you to kill yourself. So who is the author of this thought? It is from Satan, your unseen enemy.

Let's say that you wake up one morning with the sudden thought: *This is a terrible day. Everything will fall apart. It's hopeless.* Is this wisdom "pure"? Is it "peace loving, considerate...full of mercy and good fruit"? Of course it is not. Then, it is not wisdom from above. This kind of thought is from your unseen enemy.

The Apostle Paul gave us the standard for our thoughts:

> Finally, brethren, whatsoever things are true, whatsoever things are honest, whatsoever things are just, whatsoever things are pure, whatsoever things are lovely, whatsoever things are of good report; if there be any virtue, and if there be any praise, think on these things.
> Philippians 4:8 (KJV)

How to Shut off Ungodly Thoughts

The more we become familiar with the Bible and stay in communion with God, the more we can identify the sources of wisdom that come to us. Then we must learn how to shut off the ungodly channels.

If you are receiving wisdom from the enemy, you can stop it. Simply command him, "I bind you and command you to stop in Jesus' Name."

Maybe your mind is telling you something contrary to the Bible. Speak to yourself, saying:

> God's Word promises in 1 Corinthians 2:16 that I "have the mind of Christ." Mind, I command you to line up with the Word. You will not think such thoughts. According to 2 Corinthians 10:5, I "demolish arguments and every pretension that sets itself up against the knowledge of God." I "take captive every thought to make it obedient to Christ," in Jesus' Name.

Perhaps you are hearing from your flesh. You can break lustful thoughts instantly. For example, if your eyes are looking at something that is not good, say:

> Eyes, I am dead in Jesus Christ. You will not subject me to lust again, in Jesus' Name, because it has no power over me.

In a later chapter, I will show you in more detail how to submit your mind and flesh to the Lord. Right now, let me say this: Although many have tried, we cannot overcome our flesh with our wills. This is impossible. We will never win by trying harder. We win through the death of Jesus Christ. This is the source of our power. This is how we achieve victory over the lust of the flesh, the lust of the eyes, and the pride of life.

Reckon yourself indeed dead unto sin. Confess this again:

> I have been crucified with Christ and I no longer live,
> but Christ lives in me. The life I live in the body, I live by
> faith in the Son of God, who loved me and gave himself
> for me.
>
> Galatians 2:20

Do not allow the enemy's words to limit you any longer.
Remember, if you are a Christian, Jesus Himself has seated you
at His "right hand in the heavenly places, far above all
principality, and power, and might, and dominion, and every
name that is named" (Ephesians 1:18-23, KJV).

Instead, proclaim:

> Satan, you cannot get to me except through Colossians
> 3:3 (KJV). It says that I am dead and my "life is hid with
> Christ in God." So you have to go through God to get to me.

Control Your Words

You know how to tune into the channel of God's Word and
connect to the right source. You have set your channel selector
on the right channel. Now, you can take the next step to
conquering your unseen enemies.

Once you have identified the source of your thoughts, you
need to curb your tongue. Do not try to stop your tongue until
you stop the thoughts, because you only will become angry
with yourself and bite your tongue! This is very frustrating. I
know people who become upset with themselves, because they
continually speak wrong words.

The tongue can be a very destructive entity.

> We all stumble in many ways. If anyone is never at
> fault in what he says, he is a perfect man, able to keep his

whole body in check.

When we put bits into the mouths of horses to make them obey us, we can turn the whole animal.

Or take ships as an example. Although they are so large and are driven by strong winds, they are steered by a very small rudder wherever the pilot wants to go.

Likewise the tongue is a small part of the body, but it makes great boasts. Consider what a great forest is set on fire by a small spark.

The tongue also is a fire, a world of evil among the parts of the body. It corrupts the whole person, sets the whole course of his life on fire, and is itself set on fire by hell.

James 3:2-6

When we control our thoughts and tongues, we can turn the course of people's lives. The same tongue that can bring destruction also can bring eternal life and deliverance to a person. We can declare God's Word, which brings life and understanding. Or we can propagate the devil's destruction.

Do not "say what you think." Instead, consider your thoughts before you speak a word! You cannot afford to say what you think. Instead, you must identify the source first. Ask yourself if your thoughts line up with the Word. Only speak them if they do.

Of course, to do this you must keep the Word of God in your mind and heart continually and stay in constant communion with God. Otherwise, you will not know the standard to measure your thoughts against. Remember, if you continually read and meditate on God's Word, you will stay in His presence. Then, His blessings will overtake your life (Joshua 1:7-9).

Break Evil Words

If you or other people speak evil words against you, you

must condemn those words. Do this by proclaiming the Word of God over your life. Quote the following verse:

> No weapon that is formed against thee shall prosper; and every tongue that shall rise against thee in judgment thou shalt condemn. This is the heritage of the servants of the LORD, and their righteousness is of me, saith the LORD.
>
> Isaiah 54:17 (KJV)

Have you ever felt like David did when he cried out for deliverance in Psalm 64?

> ...Hear me, O God, as I voice my complaint; protect my life from the threat of the enemy.
>
> Hide me from the conspiracy of the wicked, from that noisy crowd of evildoers.
>
> who sharpen their tongues like swords and aim their words like deadly arrows.
>
> They shoot from ambush at the innocent man; they shoot at him suddenly, without fear.
>
> They encourage each other in evil plans, they talk about hiding their snares; they say, "Who will see them?"
>
> They plot injustice and say, "We have devised a perfect plan!" Surely the mind and heart of man are cunning.
>
> Psalm 64:1-6

What is God's response?

> But God will shoot them with arrows; suddenly they will be struck down.
>
> He will turn their own tongues against them and

bring them to ruin; all who see them will shake their heads in scorn.

All mankind will fear; they will proclaim the works of God and ponder what he has done.

Let the righteous rejoice in the LORD and take refuge in him; let all the upright in heart praise him!

Psalm 64:7-10

Take encouragement from the Bible. Declare that God is your refuge, and praise Him.

You Are a Love Child

The Word explains what your responsibility is toward those who harm you:

Do not repay anyone evil for evil. Be careful to do what is right in the eyes of everybody.

If it is possible, as far as it depends on you, live at peace with everyone.

Do not take revenge, my friends, but leave room for God's wrath, for it is written: "It is mine to avenge; I will repay," says the Lord.

On the contrary: "If your enemy is hungry, feed him; if he is thirsty, give him something to drink. In doing this, you will heap burning coals on his head."

Do not be overcome by evil, but overcome evil with good.

Romans 12:17-21

The proper godly response is to love your enemies.

You might say, *But you don't know what that person did to me. How can I walk in love? Even if I wanted to, I don't know how to do it.*

113

Within you, you already have the ability to love. The Word says that God lives in you:

> And we have seen and testify that the Father has sent his Son to be the Savior of the world.
> If anyone acknowledges that Jesus is the Son of God, *God lives in him and he in God.*
> And so we know and rely on the love God has for us. *God is love.* Whoever lives in love lives in God, and God in him.
>
> 1 John 4:14-16

This passage declares that God lives in you and you in Him. The very nature of God is love, right? You are born of God, right? Then, *your* spiritual nature is love, as God's is! I want you to know and believe that you are a love child. You are born of love.

Therefore, loving people is very easy! Are you surprised? Do not be. The enemy tries to deceive you into thinking it is hard to love people.

The Bible says that if we are born of God, we automatically love others who also are born of God:

> Everyone who believes that Jesus is the Christ is born of God, and everyone who loves the father loves his child as well.
>
> 1 John 5:1

We, as Christians, also love God. The Bible explains why:

> We love him [God], because he first loved us.
>
> 1 John 4:19 (KJV)

Now, love is our nature, because it is His nature.

...God has poured out his love into our hearts by the Holy Spirit, whom he has given us.

Romans 5:5

Love gushes from me all the time. There is never a time when I will fail to love you. It is impossible. Why? My nature is love, and so is yours—if you are a Christian. To conquer your unseen enemies and walk in victory, you must believe that the nature of love is inside you and that you cannot quit loving. Nothing will be able to stop you from loving, because you are born of love.

Now, it is up to you and me to take this love to a hurting world.

Beloved, if God so loved us, we ought also to love one another.

1 John 4:11 (KJV)

The Final Word

This is my prayer for you:

For this reason, since the day we heard about you, we have not stopped praying for you and asking God to fill you with the knowledge of his will through all spiritual wisdom and understanding.

And we pray this in order that you may live a life worthy of the Lord and may please him in every way: bearing fruits in every good work, growing in the knowledge of God.

Colossians 1:9-10

11
GO! in God's Power and Authority

Christ has equipped His Church with the necessary tools to conquer our unseen enemies. In this chapter, we will complete our discussion about these tools and learn what our Lord expects of His Body.

We Have the Power of the Holy Spirit

When God made us new creations in Jesus Christ, He gave the power of the Holy Spirit to us. As I briefly mentioned in the first section of this book, Jesus promised:

> But ye shall receive power, after that the Holy Ghost is come upon you: and ye shall be witnesses unto me both in Jerusalem, and in all Judaea, and in Samaria, and unto the uttermost part of the earth.
>
> Acts 1:8 (KJV)

Here, Jesus said that we would "receive power."

John wrote, referring to the Holy Spirit:

> You, dear children, are from God and have overcome them, because *the one who is in you is greater than the one who is in the world.*
>
> 1 John 4:4

Jesus quoted Isaiah 61:1-2 when He said:

The Spirit of the Lord is upon me, because he hath anointed me to preach the gospel to the poor; he hath sent me to heal the brokenhearted, to preach deliverance to the captives, and recovering of sight to the blind, to set at liberty them that are bruised,

To preach the acceptable year of the Lord.

And he began to say unto them, This day is this scripture fulfilled in your ears.

Luke 4:18-19, 21 (KJV)

The anointing, or the power of the Holy Spirit, breaks the yoke of evil.

...The yoke shall be destroyed because of the anointing.

Isaiah 10:27 (KJV)

Jesus cast out devils by the power of the Spirit of God. He said:

But if *I drive out demons by the Spirit of God,* then the kingdom of God has come upon you.

Matthew 12:28

It is by the same Holy Spirit that we, too, can cast out demons. God has given *power* to us to conquer our unseen enemies, and nothing can stand against us:

And the seventy returned again with joy, saying, Lord, even the devils are subject unto us through thy name.

And he [Jesus] said unto them, I beheld Satan as lightning fall from heaven.

Behold, I give unto you *power to tread on serpents and scorpions, and over all the power of the enemy: and nothing shall by any means hurt you.*

Luke 10:17-19 (KJV)

Jesus Delegated His Authority

Jesus not only gave *power* to His disciples and to us, but He also delegated His *authority*. What power and authority did He have?

And having disarmed the powers and authorities, he [Jesus] made a public spectacle of them, triumphing over them by the cross.

Colossians 2:15

Remember, since Jesus delegated it to us, we now have power *and* authority over demons and their activities:

When Jesus had called the Twelve together, he gave them *power and authority to drive out all demons* and to cure diseases,
and he sent them out to preach the kingdom of God and to heal the sick.

Luke 9:1-2

God ordained the Church to have dominion and power over every demon. You and I share in that dominion over the enemy.

It is one kind of experience to witness door-to-door in Christianized, civilized nations. It is another to declare Jesus Christ as Lord in nations where fetish worshipers perform magic, and then see the "Greater One" rise up to bring the whole tribe to Christ! I have seen this happen. This is the power and authority of God in action through His children.

How does authority work? As an example, let's consider a policewoman. If a tractor-trailer were to roll down the road, and a five-feet-two-inch policewoman were to stand in the street and blow her whistle, that truck driver would stop. However, if someone else were to stand in the road trying to stop traffic, the vehicles would zoom past. What is the difference between the little woman and the second person? The little woman wears a uniform that represents *authority*. She represents the government, which made the laws that she enforces.

It is because of God's authority delegated to Jesus that the earth comes under subjection. This is also true of the spiritual realm. It is not because of might and strength. It is because of the authority that God has given to Jesus through the Holy Spirit.

> Not by might, nor by power, but by my spirit, saith the LORD of hosts.
>
> Zechariah 4:6b (KJV)

As believers, you and I have the same authority of Jesus through the Holy Spirit. When we speak, it is God speaking through the Holy Spirit. Demons have to listen to you, as if God were talking. How do they respond to God?

> Thou believest that there is one God; thou doest well: the devils also believe, and tremble.
>
> James 2:19 (KJV)

Similarly, demons tremble in the face of Jesus' authority when you know how to use it. The physical and spiritual realms must yield to the authority of Jesus in you.

Clothed with Supernatural Armor

In this chapter, we have learned that God has given His Spirit to us and has delegated His power and authority to us. However, this is not all. God also has clothed us with Himself. We have His armor to wear. The Bible says:

- "...So let us put aside the deeds of darkness and put on the armor of light" (Romans 13:12).
- "Put on the full armor of God so that you can take your stand against the devil's schemes" (Ephesians 6:11).
- "...Approving ourselves as the ministers of God...by the armour of righteousness..." (2 Corinthians 6:4, 7, KJV).

God has clothed us with His armor. Now, when we fight the devil, we do it in God's strength, using His weapons and defenses, not ours. Let's more carefully examine the passage in Ephesians:

Put on the full armor of God so that you can take your stand against the devil's schemes.

For our struggle is not against flesh and blood, but against the rulers, against the authorities, against the powers of this dark world and against the spiritual forces of evil in the heavenly realms.

Therefore put on the full armor of God, so that when the day of evil comes, you may be able to stand your ground, and after you have done everything, to stand.

Stand firm then, with the belt of truth buckled around your waist, with the breastplate of righteousness in place,

and with your feet fitted with the readiness that comes from the gospel of peace.

121

In addition to all this, take up the shield of faith, with which you can extinguish all the flaming arrows of the evil one.

Take the helmet of salvation and the sword of the Spirit, which is the word of God.

And pray in the Spirit on all occasions with all kinds of prayers and requests. With this in mind, be alert and always keep on praying for all the saints.

Ephesians 6:11-18

Even this is not all that God has given to us. The devil already is running scared, but there is more!

Defeat Satan in Jesus' Name

Jesus is alive and powerful. So is His Name!

...Fear not; I am the first and the last:

I am he that liveth, and was dead; and, behold, I am alive for evermore, Amen; and have the keys of hell and of death.

Revelation 1:17-18 (KJV)

God also has given the Name of Jesus to us. As we read earlier, the Bible says that Jesus' Name is above every name. When He rose from the dead, God gave to Him the Name that is above all names:

And being found in fashion as a man, he humbled himself, and became obedient unto death, even the death of the cross.

Wherefore God also hath highly exalted him, and

given him *a name which is above every name:*

That at the name of Jesus every knee should bow, of things in heaven, and things in earth, and things under the earth;

And that every tongue should confess that Jesus Christ is Lord, to the glory of God the Father.

Philippians 2:8-11 (KJV)

The name of a man conquered our unseen enemy! Now, all authority of God is in the Name of Jesus in the Heavens and the earth! This is why Jesus said to pray in His Name:

And whatsoever ye shall ask in my name, that will I do, that the Father may be glorified in the Son.

John 14:13 (KJV)

Our entrance to the Father is on the basis of Jesus' humanity and what He did for us as a man. Therefore, we have absolute dominion and triumph over all the works of the enemy through the power of Jesus' Name.

Through thee will we push down our enemies: through thy name will we tread them under that rise up against us.

Psalm 44:5 (KJV)

When we act in the Name of Jesus, we exercise what lawyers call *power of attorney*. This means that legally whatever we do, it is as if Jesus Himself were doing it. We operate in the full power and authority of Jesus Christ.

Let me give you an example. When my family and I lived in Tulsa, Oklahoma, we still owned a house in Delaware. Since someone else managed the home for us, we gave our power of attorney to this person. He was able to act on our behalf—that is, *in our names*—to conduct business.

You see, God gave to Jesus Christ a Name that is above every name—a Name to which all things in heaven, on earth, and under the earth must bow. Then, He gave power of attorney to man and said, "Go in My Name."

Your Response: GO!

What does His Name represent? It represents *Him*. Remember, Jesus commanded us:

> ..."Go into all the world and preach the good news to all creation.
> "Whoever believes and is baptized will be saved, but whoever does not believe will be condemned.
> "And these signs will accompany those who believe: *In my name* they will drive out demons; they will speak in new tongues;
> "they will pick up snakes with their hands; and when they drink deadly poison, it will not hurt them at all; they will place their hands on sick people, and they will get well."
>
> Mark 16:15-18

Now, since we are in Christ, we sit with Him, far above all demons and Satan:

> And ye are complete in him [Jesus], which is the head of all principality and power.
>
> Colossians 2:10 (KJV)

We must view the enemy as if we need a microscope to see his position. This is because of the authority and power that the Son of God has given to us. Remember, it is by Jesus' authority and power that we wrestle the devil and his demons.

Jesus and Satan are not equal opposites. No! Jesus already has defeated Satan. Jesus is our Victor, and He commands us to *GO* minister to others. We do this by, through, and in Jesus. We now have His authority and power to minister deliverance, healing, and love to the world.

Deliverance is very simple. We merely need to say to demons: "In the Name of Jesus, I command you to leave." We do not have to get emotional, because we are in absolute authority. We simply command the demons, and they obey our voices.

Our problem is that we do not believe it. So we say, "Excuse me, Mr. Devil. Are you listening to me?" Of course he is, but if you do not believe it, why should he obey you? Remember, Jesus said:

> And these signs will accompany those who believe:
> In my name they will drive out demons....
> Mark 16:17

You have the *power* and the *authority* of Jesus Christ in you to cast out demons. Remember what these words mean:

- *Power* is the ever-present, explosive, life-giving force of God's ability.
- *Authority* is God's *power* with His legal right to use it!

God's power and authority are now yours! What are you doing with this ability?

Jesus said, "Go!" Where are we to go? We must go to wherever people are hurting in spiritual blindness and confusion, and to wherever disease and afflictions of the enemy are. That is where we are to go. We must find the serpents and scorpions, and then walk on them! We must conquer the unseen enemies. That is why God has given this powerful tool to us. It is not for us to use merely on our own needs. No, Jesus has called us to GO—to heal and deliver those who are hurting!

Part 3

Destroy
the Deeds
of
Darkness

12
Discover the *Real* Truth about Satan

Before we can engage in spiritual warfare to destroy the deeds of darkness, we must understand our enemy. Who is he? What is his name? What aliases does he use? Where did he come from? What will be his end? How did he become our enemy? What is his plan? Where does he live? What are his characteristics? What does he know? Who are his troops?

In this chapter, you will learn the answers to these questions and more. We will begin to unravel the lies many believe about our unseen enemy, Satan. The truth is he is not all-powerful but is a defeated foe.

Know the Enemy

In war, military leaders must understand their enemies' locations and operations. This is very important in preparing an offense and defense. America has invested heavily in surveillance, so we can understand our potential enemies. As Christians, we need surveillance, too. It is critical that we know where and how our enemies operate. Otherwise, our adversaries, Satan and his demons, will catch us unaware.

> Lest Satan should get an advantage of us: for we are not ignorant of his devices.
>
> 2 Corinthians 2:11 (KJV)

In modern times, the Church as a whole has been unaware

of the tactics of our unseen enemies. This lack of knowledge can destroy us. As the industrialized nations continue to develop, they drift further than ever from the Bible's truths. Yes, Satan is a real angel. Yes, demons are knowing beings with evil natures, and their purpose is to destroy you!

> My people are destroyed for lack of knowledge....
> Hosea 4:6 (KJV)

From my testimony in the beginning of this book, you will recall that, at one point, my mother knew what my problem was. She said that I had evil spirits. However, she did not have enough knowledge to set me free. So she took me to someone with more knowledge and the gifts of the Holy Spirit. There, God delivered me.

The correct knowledge of our unseen enemies is vital. This is the first lesson of warfare: Know your enemy.

What Is His Name?

Our enemy is Satan. Who is Satan?

The Scriptures mention Satan more than two hundred times. His names include:

- The prince of the power of the air (Ephesians 2:2, KJV)
- The god of this world (2 Corinthians 4:4, KJV)
- The prince of this world (John 12:31, 14:30, 16:11)
- The prince of the devils (Matthew 9:34, 12:24; Mark 3:22, KJV)
- A king (Revelation 9:11)
- The anointed cherub (Ezekiel 28:14, KJV)
- An angel of light (2 Corinthians 11:14)
- Morning star (Isaiah 14:12, NIV)

- Son of the morning or dawn (Isaiah 14:12, KJV, NIV)
- Lucifer (Isaiah 14:12, KJV)
- The devil (John 8:44; Ephesians 6:11; Hebrews 2:14; 1 Peter 5:8; 1 John 3:8; Revelation 12:9, 20:2)
- Serpent (Genesis 3:1; Isaiah 27:1; Revelation 12:9, 20:2)
- Our adversary (1 Peter 5:8, KJV)
- The accuser of the brethren (Revelation 12:10, KJV)
- Our enemy (Genesis 3:15; 1 Peter 5:8, NIV; Matthew 13:39; Luke 10:19)
- The tempter (Matthew 4:3; 1 Thessalonians 3:5)
- The oppressor (Isaiah 51:13)
- The wicked one (Matthew 13:19, 13:38-39, KJV; 1 John 2:13, 5:18, KJV)
- The thief (John 10:1,10)
- A murderer (John 8:44)
- A roaring lion (1 Peter 5:8)
- A liar (John 8:44)
- The father of lies (John 8:44, NIV)

This is only a sampling of Satan's names in the Bible. Notice how each name declares his nature or activity.

Satan's Glorious Beginning

Ezekiel described Satan's beginning, when his name was Lucifer:

> ..."'You were the model of perfection,
>   full of wisdom and perfect in beauty.
> You were in Eden,
>   the garden of God;
> every precious stone adorned you:

> ruby, topaz and emerald, chrysolite, onyx and
> jasper, sapphire, turquoise and beryl.
> Your settings and mountings were made of gold;
>   on the day you were created they were prepared.
> You were anointed as a guardian cherub,
>   for so I ordained you.
> You were on the holy mount of God;
>   you walked among the fiery stones.'"
>
> Ezekiel 28:12-14

You see, originally God had created Lucifer as a beautiful, worshiping angel, who covered the throne of God with praise and glory. Lucifer gave majesty to the King! In fact, he had musical instruments within him for this purpose:

> ...The workmanship of thy tabrets [a kind of musical instrument] and of thy pipes was prepared in thee in the day that thou wast created.
>
> Ezekiel 28:13 (KJV)

An anointed cherub, Lucifer was not a puny weakling with pudgy cheeks and a halo. No, he was a powerful, glorious, and wise creature.

Satan Sinned

Yet, his glory and splendor were not enough. Satan sinned. Ezekiel continued (in the King James Version):

> Thou wast perfect in thy ways from the day that thou wast created, till *iniquity was found in thee.*
> By the multitude of thy merchandise they have *filled*

the midst of thee with violence, and thou hast sinned.
Ezekiel 28:15-16a (KJV)

Here, we read that Satan originated sin. You see, sin existed before God ever created man. Man did not originate sin. Satan authored sin; he sinned from the beginning. Man simply accepted Satan's sin nature.

Let's examine how the devil first sinned. What was he thinking?

> "'Your heart became *proud*
>   on account of your beauty,
> and *you corrupted your wisdom*
>   because of your splendor.'"
Ezekiel 28:17a

> You said in your heart,
>   "I *will* ascend to heaven;
> I *will* raise my throne
>   above the stars of God;
> I *will* sit enthroned on the mount of assembly,
>   on the utmost heights of the sacred mountain.
> I *will* ascend above the tops of the clouds;
>   I *will* make myself like the Most High."
Isaiah 14:13-14

You see, Satan has willpower. He can choose, and he chose to sin. The adversary fell into pride, because God had created him as a very beautiful and splendid being. However, Satan desired a higher position. He wanted to rule the angelic host of God.

Because of his sin nature, Satan lost his natural wisdom, his ability to perceive correctly. He lost sight of his glorious position that he already had in Heaven. In fact, Satan already sat above the stars of God. No other angel had such great power. However, when he had allowed iniquity to work within him, the Bible says that Satan's wisdom became corrupted. He lost his perspective of what was true and real.

Think about it. Why would anyone in the position that the adversary held before his fall seek greater exaltation? There would be no cause for it. However, when the sin nature arose in him, Satan became deceived. He aspired to be God and to sit at the head of the Church.

God Cast Satan from Heaven

Because of this sin nature and his rebellion, God banished Satan from Heaven and cast him to the earth.

> "'So I drove you in disgrace from the mount of God,
>   and I expelled you, O guardian cherub,
>   from among the fiery stones.
> *So I threw you to the earth;*
>   I made a spectacle of you before kings.'"
>
> Ezekiel 28:16b, 17b

Heaven is where Satan first lived. Earth is where he came to dwell. Another description of the enemy's fall is in the book of Isaiah.

> How you have fallen from heaven,
>   O morning star [Lucifer], son of the dawn!
> You have been *cast down to the earth*,
>   you who once laid low the nations!
>
> Isaiah 14:12

Today, Satan and his demons roam the earth freely. They are not in Hell, yet, although they do have an appointed time of judgment. (We will discuss this shortly.) In fact, demons on earth in Christ's time still are on the earth today, inhabiting the bodies of people who give place to them.

Ruler of the Air

Often, people misunderstand Satan and his positions in the earth and Heaven. Some people think he is still in Heaven, while others believe he is in Hell. Here, we see that Satan fell from Heaven to the earth.

Where on earth does Satan dwell, now? Let's look at what the Apostle Paul wrote in Ephesians 2. (Although we examined these verses in an earlier chapter, I want to focus on different aspects, here.) Speaking of their lives before accepting Christ, Paul addressed the Ephesians:

> As for you, you were dead in your transgressions and sins,
> in which you used to live when you followed the ways of this world and of the *ruler of the kingdom of the air,* the spirit who is now at work in those who are disobedient.
>
> Ephesians 2:1-2

Notice, there is one ruler of the kingdom of the air. His name is Satan. His present dwelling place is in the atmosphere around the earth. Paul continued:

> All of us also lived among them [those who are disobedient] at one time, gratifying the cravings of our

135

sinful nature and following its desires and thoughts. Like the rest, we were by nature objects of wrath.

Ephesians 2:3

The Amplified Bible translates these first two verses as follows:

And you [He made alive], when you were dead [slain] by [your] trespasses and sins

In which at one time you walked habitually. You were following the course and fashion of this world— were under the sway of the tendency of this present age—following the prince of the power of the air. *(You were obedient to him and were under his control,) the [demon] spirit that still constantly works in the sons of disobedience—* the careless, the rebellious and the unbelieving, who go against the purposes of God.

Ephesians 2:1-2 (AMP)

Satan is the god of this world, the earth. He has tremendous power to control the lost human race through the sin nature. Our invisible enemy is not some little fly. No, we are dealing with a strong angel, one who used to have dominion over humanity from Adam until Jesus appeared.

Where Did Demons Originate?

Satan sinned, God cast him and one-third of the angels from Heaven. These beings—once angels of God—became demons, or evil spirits. They are fallen angels, not spirits of dead people or offspring of angels and men, as some suppose. The book of Revelation explains:

Then another sign appeared in heaven: an enormous red dragon with seven heads and ten horns and seven crowns on his heads.

His tail swept a third of the stars out of the sky and flung them to the earth.

Revelation 12:3-4

Here, we see that when Satan fell, a third of the "stars" came from Heaven with him. In this instance, *stars* refer to the angels who fell. Thus, demons came into existence.

Demons Have Knowledge

It is amazing how little most people know about evil spirits. Remember, the Greek word *demon* comes from a root word *da*, which means "to know." Therefore, a demon is a knowing being with a sphere of knowledge.

Why do people go to palm readers, tea-leaf readers, tarot-card interpreters, crystal gazers, and horoscope experts? They seek knowledge. Since a demon is a knowing being, what do these mediums produce? It is merely the knowledge of demons.

Let's examine Deuteronomy 18. Part of this chapter is about the occult and false religions. These are areas in which Satan works.

When you enter the land the Lord your God is giving you, do not learn to imitate the detestable ways of the nations there.

Deuteronomy 18:9

You see, all the nations in the earth worshiped demons then. Only one nation, Israel, knew the true God. The others had idols. Continuing, we read:

Let no one be found among you who sacrifices his
son or daughter in the fire, who practices divination or
sorcery, interprets omens, engages in witchcraft,
or casts spells, or who is a medium or spiritist or who
consults the dead.
Anyone who does these things is detestable to the
LORD, and because of these detestable practices the
LORD your God will drive out those nations before you.
You must be blameless before the LORD your God.
Deuteronomy 18:10-13

Like these nations of old, some Christians today accept
satanic knowledge through satanically inspired practices. Ouija
boards, astrology, and horoscopes, for example, are tools of the
devil. People tragically say, "Oh, well, these things won't hurt
me." No, Satan is out to rob, kill, and destroy you; and he will
use everything possible to gain access into your life. Jesus
warned, speaking of Satan:

The thief comes only to steal and kill and destroy.
John 10:10a

When you use Satan's tools in your life, you open doors for him
to destroy you. With your permission, then, he can walk in and
devour your life.

Be sober, be vigilant; because your adversary the
devil, as a roaring lion, walketh about, seeking whom he
may devour.
1 Peter 5:8 (KJV)

Never forget, the devil is your adversary. His first goal is to cause you to turn from serving God and ministering the Gospel to others. Some of his tactics include tempting you to sin to discredit your Christian witness. Or he will try to handicap you severely by stealing God's blessings from you. He wants to destroy your life.

However, no matter what you do, God still will love you. Paul assured us:

> For I am persuaded, that neither death, nor life, nor angels, nor principalities, nor powers, nor things present, nor things to come,
>
> Nor height, nor depth, nor any other creature, shall be able to separate us from the love of God, which is in Christ Jesus our Lord.
>
> Romans 8:38-39 (KJV)

Hell Is for the Devil

Where did Hell come from? God created Hell from Satan's nature for Satan, not man.

> "'...So I [God] made a fire come out from you [Lucifer], and it consumed you, and I reduced you to ashes on the ground in the sight of all who were watching.
>
> All the nations who knew you are appalled at you; you have come to a horrible end and will be no more.'"
>
> Ezekiel 28:18-19

> Yet thou shalt be brought down to hell, to the sides of the pit.
>
> Isaiah 14:15 (KJV)

> Those who see you stare at you,

they ponder your fate:
"Is this the man who shook the earth
 and made kingdoms tremble,
the man who made the world a desert,
 who overthrew its cities
 and would not let his captives go home?"

Isaiah 14:16-17

Jesus said that Hell is for the devil and his angels:

Then shall he say also unto them on the left hand,
Depart from me, ye cursed, into everlasting fire, *prepared
for the devil and his angels.*

Matthew 25:41 (KJV)

God did not create Hell for mankind. He intended this
horrible place of suffering to be for Satan and his demons. The book
of Revelation explains what will become of our unseen enemies:

And I saw an angel come down from heaven, having
the key of the bottomless pit and a great chain in his hand.
 And he laid hold on the dragon, that old serpent, which
is the Devil, and Satan, and bound him a thousand years,
 And cast him into the bottomless pit, and shut him
up, and set a seal upon him, that he should deceive the
nations no more, till the thousand years should be
fulfilled: and after that he must be loosed a little season.

Revelation 20:1-3 (KJV)

Then, after a season, Satan will receive his just reward:

And the devil that deceived them was cast into the

lake of fire and brimstone, where the beast and the false
prophet are, and shall be tormented day and night for
ever and ever.

Revelation 20:10 (KJV)

Satan and his demons know they have an appointed time of
judgment. When Jesus ministered to the demoniac from the
Gadarenes, the demons cried out:

"What do you want with us, Son of God?" they
shouted. "Have you come here to torture us before the
appointed time?"

Matthew 8:29

One day, at God's appointed time, He permanently will banish
Satan and his fallen angels to Hell. However, until that time, our
enemy and his demons are free to roam the earth. Their goal is
to take as many men, women, and children to Hell with them.

Choose Heaven or Hell

Praise God that we have the Holy Spirit's conviction to help
us serve God! Since Adam's Fall, mankind has the power of
choice to follow God or Satan. Each of us will reap eternal
consequences for this decision.

You see, God pours out grace and goodness on mankind. He
sent Jesus to win eternal life back for us, so we could choose
eternal life or death. Alternatively, God pours out judgment
and wrath against Satan. When we recognize this difference in
God's intentions for man and for the devil, the Gospel becomes
clear. God desires to give salvation to humanity, not wrath.
That is good news!

141

The Devil Is Real

Let's look for a moment at how Jesus dealt with Satan. He did not talk about Satan as a figment of the imagination. No, the devil is a real being without a body. Here is an account of Jesus' interaction with a very real Satan:

> Then was Jesus led up of the spirit into the wilderness to be tempted of the devil.
>
> And when he had fasted forty days and forty nights, he was afterward an hungered.
>
> And when the tempter [Satan] came to him, he said, If thou be the Son of God, command that these stones be made bread.
>
> But he answered and said, It is written, Man shall not live by bread alone, but by every word that proceedeth out of the mouth of God.
>
> Matthew 4:1-4 (KJV)

Then, later, Matthew recorded:

> Then the devil leaveth him [Jesus], and, behold, angels came and ministered unto him.
>
> Matthew 4:11 (KJV)

Although Satan is not a flesh-and-blood person like you and me, he is real. We cannot see him or physically punch him. However, he is real nonetheless. Although he was not in flesh and blood, Satan came to Jesus as a person. The devil can move about and has the characteristics of a person such as a voice, emotions, and a will. The Bible says in various places that the devil has:

- A heart (Isaiah 14:13; Ezekiel 28:17)
- Pride (Ezekiel 28:17, NIV)
- Speech (Matthew 4:1-11; Luke 4:1-13)
- Knowledge (Job: 1:9-10; Mark 3:11-12; James 3:15)
- Power (Luke 4:6-7, KJV; Luke 10:19; Acts 26:18; 2 Corinthians 2:11; 2 Thessalonians 2:9; 2 Timothy 2:26; Hebrews 2:14)
- Desire (Isaiah 14:13-14; Matthew 12:43-45; John 8:44)
- Lusts and other passions (Ezekiel 28:11-19)

Satan is a person as you are. What makes you a person? Is it only your body? No. It is all the various aspects of your life: Spirit, will, thoughts, emotions, motivations, plans, and purposes. Satan has these. In fact, he has everything that makes up a person except a physical body.

Jesus interacted with him as a person. He dealt with the devil directly as a person. Satan spoke to Jesus, and Jesus replied. He did not say, "Satan, I do not believe you exist." Jesus waged war with the devil as a person. He used the Word of God to defeat him. So must you and I. Remember these verses:

Be sober, be vigilant; because your adversary the devil, as a roaring lion, walketh about, seeking whom he may devour:
Whom resist stedfast in the faith....
1 Peter 5:8-9 (KJV)

13
Win the War Within

Before we can wage war effectively on the kingdom of darkness, we must recognize the spiritual war raging within each of us. As we have studied, Satan and his demons can speak to your mind and tantalize the lusts of your flesh. How you handle this internal battle will determine your success in conquering your unseen enemies. In this chapter, we will discuss how to fight and win this war within you.

Can Demons Attack Christians?

Can a Christian experience problems from demons? There is a rise of teaching that says, "A Christian cannot have a demon." While it may be true that a demon cannot *possess* a born-again Christian, it surely is true that an evil spirit can *oppress* a believer. Many people use the general term *demonized* to indicate that demons are troubling a person to some degree.

For example, let's look at one of the apostles. Simon Peter declared to Jesus by divine inspiration:

> ...Thou art the Christ, the Son of the living God.
> Matthew 16:16 (KJV)

Yet, shortly afterward, this disciple made himself the mouthpiece of the devil:

> From that time forth began Jesus to show unto his

disciples, how that he must go unto Jerusalem, and suffer many things of the elders and chief priests and scribes, and be killed, and be raised again the third day.

Then Peter took him, and began to rebuke him, saying, Be it far from thee, Lord: this shall not be unto thee.

But he turned, and said unto Peter, Get thee behind me, Satan: thou art an offence unto me: for thou savourest not the things that be of God, but those that be of men.

Matthew 16:21-23 (KJV)

If Satan can put thoughts into Peter's mind—which Peter then spoke—he surely can do so with ordinary believers, today.

Consider this scenario: A Christian husband and wife are discussing their family finances. They can present two different viewpoints and can reach a rational agreement. However, suppose an evil spirit gets involved. Suddenly the wife says, "You never think of my needs!" In this case, let's say that this is not true. Here, the evil spirit created the lie and transferred it to the woman's mind. She believed this demonic source of "wisdom," then spoke the demon's words through her own mouth. Now, a giant argument takes place. The evil spirit can leave the scene, because he finished his work. The fight will rage on, perhaps for days.

Was the woman demon-possessed? No. However, for a few moments she opened herself to a subtle suggestion by that evil spirit. Then, she acted on it. As born-again Christians, we do not have Satan's nature, but evil spirits can influence us to act wrongly. That is why the Bible says:

Neither give place to the devil.

Ephesians 4:27 (KJV)

Who Is on Your Throne?

Maybe you are wondering, *How can God and the devil operate within the same person?*

Christian Only in Heart (Inward). When the Lord delivered me from the state mental hospital, I operated both in godly and worldly ways. My spiritual problem was very basic: I had received Jesus as my Savior in my heart, but I had not bowed myself to Him as Lord. When I prayed on that fateful day at the mental hospital, Jesus cleansed my sinful past and made me a new creation, a son of God. However, I still had to find and fulfill my new identity. The doctors did not know what had happened to me, and neither did I!

Most people understand how a Christian should act. I, however, did not. Many church attendees act like Christians without having been born-again. With me, the opposite was true. I was born-again, but I was not acting like a Christian.

Christian Only in Actions (Outward). Many people are content if their conduct merely appears Christian, while their hearts are far from Christ. They do not smoke or drink (at least not excessively). They do not take illegal drugs. They do not engage in sexual misbehavior. On the positive side, they attend church, perhaps sing in the choir, and associate with those on the same rung of the social ladder. While we could add other credits to this list, these people fall short of bowing to the total lordship of Jesus Christ.

The Bible warns that in the last days, many people will become hypocrites:

> Having a form of godliness, but denying the power thereof: from such turn away.
> Ever learning, and never able to come to the

knowledge of the truth.

2 Timothy 3:5, 7 (KJV)

Heart (Inward) and Actions (Outward) Should Agree. We must keep Jesus at the center of not only our actions, but also our hearts.

In psychology, the word *persona* is the outer personality or façade presented to others by an individual. The definition of this term is "the role that one assumes or displays in public or society; one's public image or personality, as distinguished from the inner self."[1]

In spiritual matters, Jesus seeks to change not merely the persona or outer façade, but also the inner person, which the Bible calls the *heart* or *spirit*. Jesus cares more about my *being* a son of God than my *acting* like a Christian. You see, I will live eternity in Hell, if I *act* like a Christian while *being* a child of the devil. However, Jesus really desires to reign in my heart both as King of all that I *am and all that I do*. He wants the same of you.

So how does Jesus obtain the throne of our hearts?

Born of the Holy Spirit

First, one must understand which part of us actually becomes born again. Jesus said:

> That which is born of the flesh is *flesh;* and that which is born of the Spirit is *spirit.*

John 3:6 (KJV)

Obviously, when a child is born *physically*, he takes on the image and likeness of his *earthly parents*. Thus, the flesh is born. However, the remainder of this verse says that the Spirit bears

148

a spirit. You see, *spiritually* when your human spirit is born by God's Holy Spirit, you become created in the image and likeness of your *Heavenly Father*. Now, you can receive all His benefits as a child of God. Satan is no longer your spiritual father. When you receive Jesus as your personal Savior, God becomes your spiritual Father.

In John, we read of Jesus:

> Yet to all who received him, to those who believed in his name, he gave the right to become children of God—
> children born not of natural descent, nor of human decision or a husband's will, but *born of God*.
> John 1:12-13

Remember, the Apostle Paul explained:

> For ye have not received the spirit of bondage again to fear; but ye have received the *Spirit of adoption*, whereby we cry, Abba, Father.
> The Spirit itself beareth witness with our spirit, that *we are the children of God*.
> Romans 8:15-16 (KJV)

These verses clearly show God is our spiritual Father.

When one becomes a child of God, that person has a new conflict: His human spirit has become born-again, but the rest of the person has not changed, yet. How can this be?

Man Is Three Parts

The answer lies in understanding that man is a three-part being:

- The **body** is the physical house of flesh and bone that man lives in while on the earth.
- The **soul** is comprised of the mind, will, and emotions.
- The human **spirit** is the re-created part of man that is born from the Holy Spirit.

You see, your body and soul submit to God differently from the way your spirit does. We briefly studied this in the chapter about the Fall of man.

Body. The Apostle Paul explained how to submit your body to God:

> Therefore, I urge you, brothers, in view of God's mercy, to *offer your bodies as living sacrifices,* holy and pleasing to God—which is your spiritual worship.
>
> Romans 12:1

The only way to submit your body to God is to sacrifice its lustful desires. Remember, Paul listed some of the lusts of the flesh:

> The acts of the sinful nature are obvious: sexual immorality, impurity and debauchery;
> idolatry and witchcraft; hatred, discord, jealousy, fits of rage, selfish ambition, dissensions, factions
> and envy; drunkenness, orgies, and the like. I warn you, as I did before, that those who live like this will not inherit the kingdom of God.
>
> Galatians 5:19-21

You can sacrifice your body's sinful lusts. We discussed this extensively in previous chapters. First, you must experience the revelation that Jesus' death to sin gives you authority over sin.

Then, you must walk in that authority, choosing to sacrifice your fleshly desires and remembering that the day Jesus died, you also died.

> Knowing this, that our old man is crucified with him, that the body of sin might be destroyed, that henceforth we should not serve sin.
>
> For he that is dead is freed from sin.
>
> Now if we be dead with Christ, we believe that we shall also live with him:
>
> Knowing that Christ being raised from the dead dieth no more; death hath no more dominion over him.
>
> For in that he died, he died unto sin once: but in that he liveth, he liveth unto God.
>
> Likewise reckon ye also yourselves to be dead indeed unto sin, but alive unto God through Jesus Christ our Lord.
>
> Let not sin therefore reign in your mortal body, that ye should obey it in the lusts thereof.
>
> Romans 6:6-12 (KJV)

When I miraculously escaped from the state mental hospital, I did not know how to submit my body to God. This is why I often acted contrary to His ways. However, I now know how to offer my body as a living sacrifice to the Lord. Doing this helps me to stay in tune with the voice of the Holy Spirit within my spirit.

Soul. On the other hand, you submit your soul to God by renewing your mind (part of your soul). You do this by hearing and meditating on the Word of God. Paul continued in Romans 12:

> Do not conform any longer to the pattern of this world, but *be transformed by the renewing of your mind.*

Then you will be able to test and approve what God's will is—his good, pleasing and perfect will.

Romans 12:2

Only when you obey this verse, can a real transformation and victory take place in your life. Then, you can conquer your unseen enemies.

The renewal process of your mind is like stripping the many layers of paint from an old chair. Removing the façade of paint reveals the true beauty of the wood. Similarly, the soul of man comes to Jesus with layers of ignorance, pride, self-centeredness, self-righteousness, and self-determination. However, after consistent confrontation with and meditation on God's Word, the once-hard layers begin to wear away.

> ...Thy servant did meditate in thy statutes.
>
> Thy testimonies also are my delight and my counsellors.
>
> ...My soul cleaveth unto the dust: quicken thou me according to thy word.
>
> I have declared my ways, and thou heardest me: teach me thy statutes.
>
> Make me to understand the way of thy precepts: so shall I talk of thy wondrous works.
>
> My soul melteth for heaviness: strengthen thou me according unto thy word.

Psalm 119:23-28 (KJV)

Remember, we read this verse in an earlier chapter:

> This book of the law shall not depart out of thy

152

mouth; but *thou shalt meditate therein day and night,* that thou mayest observe to do according to all that is written therein: for then thou shalt make thy way prosperous, and then thou shalt have good success.

Joshua 1:8 (KJV)

When I first left the mental hospital, I had not experienced the renewing of my mind. Instead, I was ignorant of the Word of God and still walked after my own fleshly desires. I did not know how God expected His sons to live. Yet, I was His son. Therefore, I acted in worldly ways. However, I then renewed my mind to God's Word and began to act according to the Spirit.

Spirit. Your spirit, on the other hand, comes to Jesus in free and hearty submission, instantly desiring only to come under the government of King Jesus forever.

If you see the evidence of the Holy Spirit's work in your life, then you are allowing your spirit to rule your body and soul. Paul described this to the Galatians:

> But the fruit of the Spirit is love, joy, peace, longsuffering, gentleness, goodness, faith,
> Meekness, temperance: against such there is no law.
> And they that are Christ's have crucified the flesh with the affections and lusts.
> If we live in the Spirit, let us also walk in the Spirit.

Galatians 5:22-25 (KJV)

Your Inward Battle

From the moment of salvation, your body and soul begin a lifelong battle with your spirit over the lordship and kingship of Jesus. As we have studied, this struggle began at the Fall of man in the Garden of Eden. Paul admonished the Galatians:

153

This I say then, Walk in the Spirit, and ye shall not fulfil the lust of the flesh.

For the flesh lusteth against the Spirit, and the Spirit against the flesh: and these are contrary the one to the other: so that ye cannot do the things that ye would [want to do].

Galatians 5:16-17 (KJV)

The apostle explained his personal inward battle:

For what I do is not the good I want to do; no, the evil I do not want to do—this I keep on doing.

Now if I do what I do not want to do, it is no longer I who do it, but it is sin living in me that does it.

So I find this law at work: When I want to do good, evil is right there with me.

For in my inner being I delight in God's law;

but I see another law at work in the members of my body, waging war against the law of my mind and making me a prisoner of the law of sin at work within my members.

Romans 7:19-23

As long as you are on the earth, you will experience this battle. However, the more you fellowship with God and yield to and obey His Word, the easier it becomes. Your spirit *can* rule over your body and soul.

Your Weapons Are Mighty

The simple reality is that while our spirits are born-again, our minds (souls) and bodies are not. If we are Christians, demons cannot *possess* our spirits. However, they can *oppress* us with wicked thoughts that amplify the voice and effects of the lusts of the flesh.

As we have studied, this can happen, if we do not prepare ourselves by spending time in God's presence and obeying Him. To avoid submitting to demonic influences, we must renew our minds and present our "bodies as living sacrifices, holy and pleasing to God." These are God's instructions to living a Spirit-ruled life (Romans 12:1-2).

You see, when you read the Bible and fellowship with God, you begin to know His will regarding your thoughts and behaviors. Then, when a thought crosses your mind that is contrary to God's ways, you can recognize it instantly as ungodly. Remember, good and bad thoughts continually cross your mind. You are responsible to recognize their sources and to act only on the ones in agreement with God's will. (See the earlier chapter on the four sources of wisdom.)

Remember, Paul taught the believers at Corinth about this warfare in their thoughts:

> For though we live in the world, *we do not wage war as the world does.*
>
> The weapons we fight with are not the weapons of the world. On the contrary, they have divine power to demolish strongholds.
>
> We demolish arguments and every pretension that sets itself up against the knowledge of God, and we take captive every thought to make it obedient to Christ.
>
> 2 Corinthians 10:3-5

Let's look at these verses in another translation:

> For though we walk in the flesh, *we do not war after the flesh:*

(For the weapons of our warfare are not carnal, but mighty through God to the pulling down of strong holds;)

Casting down imaginations, and every high thing that exalteth itself against the knowledge of God, and *bringing into captivity every thought to the obedience of Christ.*

2 Corinthians 10:3-5 (KJV)

We do not war after physical beings. The weapons of our warfare are not carnal, that is, sense-oriented. They have nothing to do with what we can see, smell, taste, touch, or hear in the physical realm. No, our weapons have to do with "casting down imaginations," and where do imaginations occur? They are in our minds. That is our battleground against our unseen enemies—the devil and his demons.

By understanding this, you are well on your way to destroying the deeds of darkness around you!

14
Unmask the Enemy

Many people unwittingly invite the devil to destroy their lives. Through unforgiveness, strife, pornography, possession of idols, dabbling in the occult, and other ungodly activities, they give their unseen enemy freedom to destroy their lives.

Before we can minister effectively in deliverance, we must see what is happening spiritually. Operating on guesswork will not work. We can never assume that something is a spirit; we must *know* for sure.

In this chapter, we will discuss how the Holy Spirit unveils the spiritual realm so you can detect demonic activity in or against a person. You will learn how to close the door to the devil and his temptations. Also, we will examine how to unmask some common spirits that attack people—even Christians.

The Gifts of the Holy Spirit

In 1 Corinthians 12, we find the spiritual gifts that God gives to His children:

> But the manifestation of the Spirit is given to every man to profit withal.
>
> For to one is given by the Spirit the word of wisdom; to another *the word of knowledge* by the same Spirit;
>
> To another faith by the same Spirit; to another the gifts of healing by the same Spirit;

To another the working of miracles; to another prophecy; to another *discerning of spirits;* to another divers kinds of tongues; to another the interpretation of tongues.

1 Corinthians 12:7-10 (KJV)

Two of these spiritual gifts operate in the detection and unveiling of demonic activity. One is the Word of Knowledge, which reveals what currently exists. The other is the Discerning of Spirits, which enables us to see into the spiritual realm. The *New International Version* translates this gift as "the ability to distinguish between spirits." It is the capacity to see, examine, scrutinize, and investigate spiritually.

There are four spiritual realms:

- God's angels
- Fallen angels or demons
- God's Holy Spirit
- Human spirits

The gift of Discerning of Spirits opens our spiritual eyes to see into these four realms. Often, this supernatural ability to see happens while praying with others, and suddenly we see a picture of something that exists in the spiritual realm. Remember, this gift unveils not only demonic spirits, but also the Holy Spirit and God's angels. The gift of Discerning of Spirits also reveals our human spirits.

Do you want the gift of the Discerning of Spirits? Ask God for it. The Bible instructs:

But eagerly desire the greater gifts. And now I will

show you the most excellent way.

1 Corinthians 12:31

Any Christian Can Detect Demons

Even Christians who do not have a special gift of Discerning of Spirits can recognize demons. We have the Spirit of God and the mind of Christ within us:

> The man without the Spirit does not accept the things that come from the Spirit of God, for they are foolishness to him, and he cannot understand them, because they are spiritually discerned.
> The spiritual man makes judgments about all things, but he himself is not subject to any man's judgment:
> "For who has known the mind of the Lord that he may instruct him?" But we have the mind of Christ.
>
> 1 Corinthians 2:14-16

Do not judge demons by sight. The Bible says that Satan disguises himself as an angel of light, and so do his ministers.

> And no wonder, for Satan himself masquerades as an angel of light.
>
> 2 Corinthians 11:14

However, God helps us to see past the devil's deceptions. Here's how:

> And there shall come forth a rod out of the stem of Jesse, and a Branch shall grow out of his roots:
> And the spirit of the LORD shall rest upon him, the

159

spirit of wisdom and understanding, the spirit of counsel and might, the spirit of knowledge and of the fear of the LORD;

And shall make him of quick understanding in the fear of the LORD: and he shall not judge after the sight of his eyes, neither reprove after the hearing of his ears:

But with righteousness shall he judge the poor, and reprove with equity for the meek of the earth: and he shall smite the earth with the rod of his mouth, and with the breath of his lips shall he slay the wicked.

And righteousness shall be the girdle of his loins, and faithfulness the girdle of his reins.

Isaiah 11:1-5 (KJV)

We studied earlier that our born-again human spirits sit with Jesus at the right hand of the Father, far above all principalities, power, might, and dominion. Therefore, our spirits can detect demons, because of this position of fellowship with God. Jesus said about us:

Ye are the light of the world. A city that is set on an hill cannot be hid.

Matthew 5:14 (KJV)

Thus, because the light of God's presence is in our spirits, we often can sense the source of various manifestations.

For example, have you ever walked into a store, where someone came behind you, and you felt something evil nearby? That is because your spirit is in fellowship with God, and it detects demonic activity.

We are more sensitive to the spiritual realm than we realize.

The Christian human spirit hears from God. It is in permanent fellowship with the Lord of light. Therefore, it can detect darkness. Stop rehearsing doubt by saying that you are not sensitive to the Spirit or that you fail to hear from God. Also, do not be afraid of making a mistake.

Many times I minister deliverance without the gifts of the Holy Spirit operating in clear Words of Knowledge or Discerning of Spirits. You see, my spirit is sensitive to the spiritual realm. When people come to prayer lines for ministry, I listen for the Lord's voice and allow my spirit to be sensitive to the spiritual environment. I may not have revelation of any specific problem, but my spirit tells me that darkness is present. I recognize that the people are bound. So I know the avenue in which to minister to them.

Be Sensitive, Then Act

To become sensitive to the voice of the Holy Spirit, you must stay in daily intimate fellowship with the Lord. You do this by reading the Word of God, praising Him, praying, and spending quiet time before God. Pray both in your known language and in the Holy Spirit; then wait for the interpretation.

> He that speaketh in an unknown tongue edifieth himself.
>
> 1 Corinthians 14:4a (KJV)

> But ye, beloved, building up yourselves on your most holy faith, praying in the Holy Ghost.
>
> Jude 1:20 (KJV)

> Wherefore let him that speaketh in an unknown

tongue pray that he may interpret.

1 Corinthians 14:13 (KJV)

Your heavenly Father wants to give revelation knowledge to you. He is not trying to keep you uninformed. No, God wants to reveal His plans and ways to you.

And Jesus answered and said unto him, Blessed art thou, Simon Barjona: for flesh and blood hath not revealed it unto thee, but my Father which is in heaven.

Matthew 16:17 (KJV)

God also desires to expose the devil's strategies to you, so you can destroy his works.

Sometimes, we experience what I call an "inward knowing." When this happens, we do not hear a voice or get a mental picture. Instead, we merely have an inner witness that something is not right or that evil is present.

When the Holy Ghost reveals demonic activity to you, be sure to respond aggressively. For example, people often approach me, saying, "Gary, I believe there's a demon in my home!"

"What have you done about it?" I ask.

"Well, I came to tell you."

"Don't tell *me*," I reply. "What am I going to do with it? The Holy Ghost showed it to you. Now, *you* do something about it. Cast it out in Jesus' Name!"

Sometimes we encounter religious spirits, exalting themselves against the knowledge of God's Word. If we are not in communication with the Holy Spirit, we are in danger of other voices influencing us. We must be aware of danger in the religious area. This happened even to the Apostle Paul:

> And it came to pass, as we went to prayer, a certain
> damsel possessed with a spirit of divination met us,
> which brought her masters much gain by soothsaying:
> The same followed Paul and us, and cried, saying,
> *These men are the servants of the most high God, which show*
> *unto us the way of salvation.*
>
> Acts 16:16-17 (KJV)

If we stopped here, we would think this girl was sensitive to the
Holy Spirit. Today, we would think, *Get her on TV! She could be*
a forerunner.

Was she speaking the truth in verse 17? Yes, apparently it was
true. However, what was the source of the saying? It was a demon!

> And this did she many days. But Paul, being grieved,
> turned and said to the spirit, I command thee in the name
> of Jesus Christ to come out of her. And he came out the
> same hour.
>
> Acts 16:18 (KJV)

Sometimes we can be in the presence of demonic activity for
many days and not have a revelation about what is happening.
Yet, we know something does not feel right. Suddenly one day,
we know it is a demon! Then, we can deal with it. Now, we do
not have to know the name of the demon to cast it out—only the
area of involvement. (Keep in mind that demons can lie about
their names, numbers, and strength.)

Notice that Paul did not speak to the demon by name; he
merely told it to get out. We can do the same. However, to cast

163

it out, we must recognize that it is a demon. Act quickly when you sense demons in operation.

Examine Demonic Door Openers

When dealing with demonized individuals, listen to their words. Check their sources of wisdom (which we discussed in a previous chapter). Have they been listening to human reason, the flesh, demons, or the Holy Spirit?

Are they aligned with the Word of God? If not, take them through the Scriptures, explaining what I call "demonic door openers." These are areas in people's lives that become like handles for the devil to enter the doors of their lives. If these are present, Satan has the right to enter. Whether or not the people know it, they have given place to the devil.

> As the bird by wandering, as the swallow by flying,
> so the curse causeless shall not come.
>
> Proverbs 26:2 (KJV)

My book *How to Identify and Remove Curses!* addresses this subject in detail. The devil has a right to enter our lives, when we leave the door open for him.

In ministering to others, we do not need to know by specific revelation what is happening. When we do not have clear revelation about the demonic activity present in a person's life, we can tell him how to align himself with the Word. Then, he can close any demonic door openers. If the person wants to be free, he must submit to God in the area where the Word has shown wrongdoing.

Now, let's examine a couple of examples. I will show you how to detect demonic door openers when ministering to others.

Unforgiveness. Find out if the person needs to repent of sin. For example, ask, "Is there anyone whom you have not forgiven?"

"Yes, I'll tell you—I just can't stand so-and-so," the person might respond.

First, minister to him in this area before proceeding. Explain that unforgiveness clogs God's flow of power in people's lives. The person must forgive others to release God's blessings back into his life.

Or, for example, let's say a man is bitter against his wife.

Ask him, "Have you forgiven her?"

"No!"

"Well, you need to forgive her," tell him. "If you don't get that sin out of the way, your bondage will remain. You must deal with that sin, first."

Then, quote the Word to him:

> Husbands, love your wives, even as Christ also loved the church, and gave himself for it.
>
> Ephesians 5:25 (KJV)

Help the man to recognize that he must ask the Lord to forgive him, and then return to loving his wife. Simply have him say, "I choose, in Jesus' Name, to love my wife." This is an obedient step of faith toward his deliverance.

Strife. See if the person lives in strife. For example, ask, "Do you have a lot of strife or envy around the house?"

"Oh, yes, we're always fighting over something."

If so, then minister to the person first regarding the strife. You can start by asking, "Where did you get that strife?" Then, quote what the Bible says about it:

This wisdom descendeth not from above, but is earthly, sensual, devilish.

James 3:15 (KJV)

Help the person to repent of strife, telling him that he must stop it.

Close all demonic door openers. When ministering to others, see if they have repented from these types of sin. Are they still involved with the enemy? If so, tell them that any deliverance will not last. They must submit to God's will and actively resist Satan to become free. Quote this verse:

Submit yourselves therefore to God. Resist the devil, and he will flee from you [as in terror of you!].

James 4:7 (KJV)

If you find any open doors, lead the people in prayers of repentance. Then, have them declare aloud that they are closing all doors to the enemy and that he is no longer welcome in their lives. Ask them to proclaim the above verse, stating that they are submitting to God and resisting the devil. Tell Satan that he now must flee. Remember, it is the Holy Spirit in you who drives out the demons.

Remove *Your* Demonic Door Openers

To minister effectively to others, you must remove all demonic door openers in your *own* life. If you are in rebellion to God in an area of your life, you give place to the devil. Why should your enemy listen to your commands to go when your actions allow him to stay?

Here, we will examine some common ways that people who

minister deliverance can become ensnared by the devil and be ineffective in deliverance.

Unforgiveness. Lack of forgiveness is a great stronghold of the enemy. Have you ever not wanted to forgive someone? What does God's Word say about this?

> And be ye kind one to another, tenderhearted, forgiving one another, even as God for Christ's sake hath forgiven you.
>
> Ephesians 4:32 (KJV)

Paul urged the church at Corinth to forgive others:

> Lest Satan should get an advantage of us: for we are not ignorant of his devices.
>
> 2 Corinthians 2:11 (KJV)

Unforgiveness is an operation of the devil to bind us. It entices us to hold bitterness against another person. However, the Word of God commands us:

> *Get rid of all bitterness,* rage and anger, brawling and slander, along with every form of malice.
>
> Ephesians 4:31

> *Make every effort to live in peace with all men and to be holy;* without holiness no one will see the Lord.
> See to it that no one misses the grace of God and *that no bitter root grows up to cause trouble and defile many.*
>
> Hebrews 12:14-15

If you know that you have a challenge with unforgiveness

and someone hurts you, you can defeat the devil. Say, "In the Name of Jesus and in the Person of Jesus, I forgive this person. I love him/her. I will not give you permission, Satan, to plant a root of bitterness or resentment in me." Stop that unforgiveness, right away. Do not give place to the enemy.

In my book *How to How to Identify and Remove Curses!* I included an important section on how to forgive others. If you want to walk in the power and victory of Christ, you must break the stronghold of unforgiveness in your life. Then, you can conquer your unseen enemies.

Pornography. You must resist this kind of lust. It is not a harmless private activity. No, it will try to destroy you! Pornography will invite spiritual conflict into your life. If you are married, this demon causes you to become dissatisfied with your spouse. If you are single, pornography entices you to engage in premarital sex. Even in the lives of renowned ministers of the Gospel, we have seen the tragic effects of this powerful demonic spirit.

If you struggle with this stronghold, simply confess, "Father, in Jesus' Name forgive me. Thank You for forgiving me."

Then command the demon, "Pornographic Spirit, I break your power and the spirit of adultery in Jesus' Name!"

Now you're free.

What should you do the next time you walk into a store and see that it sells pornography? Do not peek over the counter to look at those magazines. Do not give place to the enemy to influence you. Better yet, do not go to that store or any other that sells pornography!

Depression. What should you do if you wake up in the morning, with the enemy saying, "It will be a lousy day"?

You tell him, "No! It's never a lousy day in Jesus' Name! It's always a marvelous Monday, a tremendous Tuesday, a wonderful Wednesday, a terrific Thursday, or a fabulous Friday."

If you feel the spirit of despair come upon you, put on the "garment of praise":

And provide for those who grieve in Zion—to bestow on them *a crown of beauty instead of ashes, the oil of gladness instead of mourning, and a garment of praise instead of a spirit of despair.* They will be called oaks of righteousness, a planting of the LORD for the display of his splendor.

Isaiah 61:3

Many people merely exist with no enthusiasm for life. God created you to live every day in triumph! To whom will you give place? To whom will you give preeminence? Will you believe God or the devil?

Dabbling in the occult and demonic practices. Through television, movies, music, newspapers, materials at store checkouts, psychic hotlines, demonic games, and now the Internet, society bombards us with appeals to dabble in the occult and demonic practices. It is common to see materials on New Age, horoscopes, astrology, fortunetelling, witchcraft, magic, charms, crystals, handwriting analysis, palmistry, Satanism, and more.

Although some may think these are innocent activities and endeavors, the truth is they are demonic door openers. If you engage in any of these practices or possess these kinds of items, the devil has free reign in your life. You must repent and close these doors at once. Destroy and remove from your possession all materials on the occult, evil practices, evil games, and demonic beliefs. Only then can you oust the enemy from your life.

Native art and objects of devil worship. While on vacation or missionary trips, people often obtain souvenirs of native art, miniature idols or dolls, and objects of devil worship. Then, when they naively bring these demonic door openers into their homes, this releases demons to operate there.

Do you have anything like this in your home? Objects of devil worship can ensnare you, even if you are an unsuspecting Christian and do not use the objects in any form of worship.

This is as true today as it was in the times of the Bible. Concerning the handling of their defeated heathen enemies, God commanded the children of Israel:

> The images of their gods you are to burn in the fire. Do not covet the silver and gold on them, and do not take it for yourselves or you will be ensnared by it, for it is detestable to the LORD your God.
>
> Deuteronomy 7:25

Sometimes when I visit foreign countries, people want to give native art to me. I examine the art and pray over it to determine whether God wants me to have it. Most of the time I say, "No, thank you." Or, if this would be offensive, I accept the gifts then destroy them.

One time in Panama, some people wanted to give carved little dolls to us. They were cute. However, I realized that local spiritists often cast spirits into dolls like these. Our well-meaning hosts asked, "Would you like to take one of these home with you?"

"No, thank you!" I replied, thinking, *I don't want to bring an abomination into my home so my family will get sick, diseased, tormented, and confused!*

God continued His instructions to the Israelites:

Do not bring a detestable thing into your house or you, like it, will be set apart for destruction. Utterly abhor and detest it, for it is set apart for destruction.

Be careful to follow every command I am giving you today, so that you may live and increase and may enter and possess the land that the LORD promised on oath to your forefathers.

Deuteronomy 7:26-8:1

These are not *my* ideas. This is the Word of God. If you violate it, there are negative consequences that you probably will not like! To be free of demonic influence and to minister to others, you must obey His commands.

Looking for personal gain. Sometimes when ministering to others, Satan will try to trick you into asking, *What's in this for me?*

Do not yield to this temptation. Remember, you are a servant of the Most High God. You do His will, not your own. When you take care of His business, God takes care of yours. Do not look for your own satisfaction or gratification. Instead, you be obedient, and God will give to you true happiness, fulfillment, and everything you have need of. Jesus promised:

But seek ye first the kingdom of God, and his right-eousness; and all these things shall be added unto you.

Matthew 6:33 (KJV)

If you have had any demonic door openers in your life, repent now. Turn from these sins and be free in Jesus' Name!

Accusations about Your Forgiven Past

Do you believe that your past sins, for which you honestly

have confessed and repented, currently have a negative spiritual effect in your life?

If your answer is "Yes," that is a false accusation. While earthly consequences for confessed sin remain, God removes the spiritual penalty. However, Satan is a deceiver. He will try to make you believe that your past sins now prevent your fellowship with God and your victory in Jesus. If you believe that, you are letting the devil lie to you. The Bible declares:

> If we confess our sins, he is faithful and just to forgive us our sins, and to cleanse us from all unrighteousness.
>
> 1 John 1:9 (KJV)

Because Jesus is our Mediator in the New Covenant, God says:

> "For I will forgive their wickedness and will remember their sins no more."
>
> Hebrews 8:12

> As far as the east is from the west, so far hath he removed our transgressions from us.
>
> Psalm 103:12 (KJV)

These verses prove that when you confess and repent of your sins, God restores your fellowship with Him. However, this by no means is license to sin, for the Apostle Paul admonished:

> What shall we say then? Shall we continue in sin, that grace may abound?
> God forbid. How shall we, that are dead to sin, live

any longer therein?

Being then made free from sin, ye became the servants of righteousness.

Romans 6:1-2, 18 (KJV)

We simply must avoid sin and live holy lives, which are pleasing to God.

Keep Yourself

You see, our human spirits can stay free from demonic oppression. God designed us to live that way. Do not accept defeat. Keep yourself free from your enemy's influence.

We know that whosoever is born of God *sinneth not;* but he that is begotten of God *keepeth himself,* and that *wicked one toucheth him not.*

1 John 5:18 (KJV)

Remember, once you become spiritually alert, Satan cannot enter your life, unless you give him an opportunity.

Recognize that Jesus has given to you the ability to overcome the devil through the power of His mighty Name. Remember the verse we just reviewed:

Submit yourselves therefore to God. Resist the devil, and he will flee from you [as in terror of you!].

James 4:7 (KJV)

By living for God and keeping yourself holy, you have the power to resist the devil and command him to flee. This is very critical, if you minister deliverance. The devil must not have an open door into *your* life.

Resist Aggressively

Use the Word. If you need to overcome an area of challenge, speak God's Word. Remember, this is how Jesus triumphed when Satan tempted Him three times:

> But he [Jesus] answered and said, It is written, Man shall not live by bread alone, but by every word that proceedeth out of the mouth of God.
>
> Jesus said unto him, It is written again, Thou shalt not tempt the Lord thy God.
>
> Then saith Jesus unto him, Get thee hence, Satan: for it is written, Thou shalt worship the Lord thy God, and him only shalt thou serve.
>
> Matthew 4:4, 7, 10 (KJV)

The devil finally left Jesus alone.

I encourage you to do this:

- Write down pertinent Scripture verses on three-by-five cards.
- Place these cards on the dashboard of your car, your bathroom mirror, your desk at home or work, or your refrigerator.
- Then, several times each day, read those verses aloud. By doing this, you are telling yourself, the devil, his demons, and God that you are standing on God's promises for your answer.

This strengthens your spirit man to endure temptation, tells the devil and his demons that you give him no place, and builds your faith to trust God daily to perform His Word in your life.

Praise the Lord. Praising God is a powerful weapon against the enemy. In the Bible, an evil spirit departed from Saul when David played his music and praised God:

> And it came to pass, when the evil spirit from God was upon Saul, that David took an harp, and played with his hand: so Saul was refreshed, and was well, and the evil spirit departed from him.
>
> 1 Samuel 16:23 (KJV)

Consider another example in the Old Testament in which praise was a great weapon. When King Jehoshaphat sent the praise-and-worship team ahead in battle, God ambushed Israel's enemy:

> And when he had consulted with the people, he appointed singers unto the LORD, and that should praise the beauty of holiness, as they went out before the army, and to say, Praise the LORD; for his mercy endureth for ever.
>
> And when they began to sing and to praise, the LORD set ambushments against the children of Ammon, Moab, and mount Seir, which were come against Judah; and they were smitten.
>
> 2 Chronicles 20:21-22 (KJV)

Stay in the presence of praise, because God Himself inhabits the praises of His people:

> But thou art holy, O thou that inhabitest the praises of Israel.
>
> Psalm 22:3 (KJV)

Let me conclude this chapter with a discussion about several practical points in spiritual warfare.

Common Spirits

When ministering to a person, at times you will see on his face certain expressions such as depression, confusion, or fear. This does not always reflect accurately the spirits behind the problems. Check to see what you are hearing in your spirit. Also, ask the person what the Lord is showing him in his spirit. If possible, ask the person to pray in tongues with you before casting out the spirits.

Now, let's briefly look at common spirits you might face when ministering to people.

Lust. If someone has engaged in premarital or extramarital sex, indulged in pornography, or was a victim of sexual abuse, often a spirit of lust attaches itself to the person. The spirit can carry itself into the marriage to produce an abnormal frustration within that marital relationship. The one who has had premarital or extramarital sex, has been abused, or has an appetite for pornography needs to be set free. Please note that this spirit also can attach itself to the children of that marriage.

Division. The same spirits that divided a first marriage will operate in the second marriage unless the person receives deliverance. Some people refer to this as "the spirit of alienation of affection." Have you ever known people who, in two or three marriages, experience exactly the same problems over and over? Why? It is the same spirit. The marriage partners never became free.

Rejection. A spirit of rejection will play the same story over and over in someone's mind. In this way, it can sabotage every relationship a person has until he receives deliverance.

For example, let's say that a boy's mother rejects him. At that point, the spirit of rejection hooks itself into his mind. Later, he enters his first dating relationship. When the girl looks at him unusually, the spirit takes over, and he says: "I'm just unlovable. My mother rejected me. Now, you're rejecting me." Yet, somehow, he manages to get married.

The first time something goes wrong in the marriage, rejection takes over. When he goes to work, he feels that his supervisor, coworkers, or customers are rejecting him. Now, he dreads going to work. The same story plays over and over in his mind throughout his life.

Finally, the demon convinces this man that no one loves him. So, he goes to church and sits alone in a corner. He actually hopes that no one will see him, so he will not feel rejection again. Then, however, he feels rejected, because no one noticed him. It is a vicious cycle that never stops. This man needs that spirit cast out.

Fear of failure. The spirit of fear of failure can torment people—even believers. This spirit causes people to say, "That's it. I just can't go any further. Because I failed in the past, I know I'll fail again. So I might as well not try. It doesn't hurt as bad that way." The only way to turn such a person around is deliverance from that evil spirit.

Of course, there are hundreds of kinds of spirits you might need to remove. These are only a few. However, no evil spirit is greater than the Name that is above every name: the Name of Jesus.

You Cannot Cast out Some Problems

Before continuing, please note that no one can cast out certain problems. For example, we cannot cast out:

- Sin

177

- Demons that a person wants or keeps the door open for
- The flesh
- Emotions
- The personality of a person (Although we may desire to cast this out, we cannot!)
- Learned behaviors

Some actions are learned behaviors that a person must change through the knowledge of the Word. No one can cast out these problems.

Many problems are not demonic. Because of ignorance of God's Word, some Christians live like the world does. They have committed particular pet sins and continue to indulge themselves. In these cases, the devil is not making them sin. James says that people are drawn into sin by their own desire.

> But each one is tempted when, by his own evil desire, he is dragged away and enticed.
>
> James 1:14

The results are tragic, if they do not stop sinning:

> Then, after desire has conceived, it gives birth to sin; and sin, when it is full-grown, gives birth to death.
> Don't be deceived, my dear brothers.
>
> James 1:15-16

Repeated submission to temptation can yield to demonic strongholds and the destruction of your life. You must avoid this. How?

When a demon first tempts you to sin, do not yield to it. Do not commit that work of the flesh. If you do and you continue, that sin opens the door to a demonic stronghold. It all starts with your yielding to a demon just one time. For example, it is impossible to:

- Become an alcoholic, if you never drink alcohol.
- Become addicted to pornography, if you never look at it.
- Commit adultery, if you never allow yourself to be alone with a person of the opposite sex.
- Have unwanted teenage pregnancies, if young people never have premarital sex.

The key is not to yield to that first temptation.

However, if you do sin, then stop immediately. Do not keep it as a pet sin. This is an open invitation for Satan's destruction. He will gain a foothold, then eagerly rip away everything you value in your life.

The benefits of overcoming the temptation to sin are well worth the effort:

> Blessed is the man that endureth temptation: for when he is tried [stood the test (NIV)], he shall receive the crown of life, which the Lord hath promised to them that love him.
>
> James 1:12 (KJV)

Once you have identified what you are dealing with in the spiritual realm, you must do something about it. Do not simply say, "Oh, I think it's a spirit!" What will you *do* with it? The remaining pages of this book will answer this question.

15
Detect Demonic Deception

Your unseen enemy's goal is to kill you! He will use every possible avenue to reach you.

Deception, one of Satan's favorite weapons, is particularly powerful. This is because when people do not recognize the cause of their problems, they do not seek the freedom that is rightfully theirs.

Disguised as "Christian," Satan's deceptive doctrines open the door for him to destroy your life, leaving you wondering why. He even will tempt you to believe that sin is acceptable! In this chapter, we will expose several of the devil's diabolical deceptions.

Demonic Doctrines

Our unseen enemy comes to defeat us with demonic doctrines.

> The Spirit clearly says that in later times some will abandon the faith and follow *deceiving spirits* and *things taught by demons.*
>
> 1 Timothy 4:1

Deception is simply the act of believing something that is not true. The King James Version translates this verse as follows:

> Now the Spirit speaketh expressly, that in the latter times some shall depart from the faith, giving heed *to*

seducing spirits, and doctrines of devils.
1 Timothy 4:1 (KJV)

The doctrines of demons lead people to believe that which is not true. The key to understanding these demonic doctrines are the words *deceiving* and *seducing*. A *deceiving* or *seducing spirit* is one that persuades a person to act disobediently. A *doctrine of devils* or *demonic doctrine* is any teaching that comes from a spirit other than the Holy Spirit.

Take responsibility to judge all teachings that you hear—even if they come from the most powerful pulpit ministry in the world. Check them out according to the Word of God and the Holy Spirit. If a teaching does not originate from God, you must set it aside. Deceptive doctrines of demons can operate anywhere, even within the Christian church.

Transcendental meditation. In cults and false religions, such as spiritism and Eastern religions, demons do everything possible to convince people that their doctrines are not harmful.

For example, let's look at transcendental meditation or TM. Some people say, "Oh, I just do TM to relax! After all, everyone needs to relax, and TM works for me. It's okay."

No, it is not okay. If you believe this, Satan is deceiving you. In transcendental meditation, you communicate with demons. It is a doctrine of devils that you MUST avoid.

Healing through witchcraft. Satan does not open the prison door for anyone. Some people say, "Well, I can get healed through witchcraft."

No, the enemy does not heal anyone really. People might have an outward manifestation of a change, but ultimately they only have further bondage. I have traveled to many countries where people had satanic "healings." Later, however, these

182

people had to seek God Himself for true healing.

Satan is never the answer to our difficulties. People in satanic-worship cults think they receive answers. However, they really do not. Instead, they submit themselves to further control of the devil.

Pet "Christian" Demonic Doctrines. Demons also promote doctrinal errors within the Body of Christ through religion, ritualism, formalism, legalism, and other unbiblical teachings.

Have you ever met people with doctrinal obsessions? They love their pet doctrines, but distort the truth of the Gospel. Often, they can quote Scripture to justify their beliefs, but beware! They twist the words of the Bible to promote their false teachings. Let's briefly look at a few examples of this.

Demons lie to us about **prosperity and poverty.** This is why many Christians—and even pastors—have problems with Christians prospering. I have heard that God does not want to prosper us, because poverty supposedly is godly. This is *not* true! The psalmist declared:

> Let them shout for joy, and be glad, that favour my righteous cause: yea, let them say continually, *Let the LORD be magnified, which hath pleasure in the prosperity of his servant.*
>
> Psalm 35:27 (KJV)

Prosperity is part of God's covenant with man:

> But thou shalt remember the LORD thy God: for *it is he that giveth thee power to get wealth, that he may establish his covenant* which he sware unto thy fathers, as it is this day.
>
> Deuteronomy 8:18 (KJV)

Poverty is a curse. In my book *How to Identify and Remove Curses!* I devote an entire chapter to reversing the curse against finances. Poverty exalts itself against the knowledge of God's Word. You see, God intends for His Word to break the yoke of poverty and release people to blessings, not keep them subjected to poverty.

Similarly, some people accept **sickness** as God's will. They say, "Well, God made me sick to get my attention and to teach a lesson to me."

This would be like a man draining all the brake fluid from his wife's or teenage daughter's car. Then, after she wrecked the car and landed in the hospital, the man would say, "Honey, I wanted you to crash. The reason is so I could talk to you." Doesn't that sound demented? Yes! Likewise, the thinking that God wants you sick to teach a lesson to you is foolish.

No, the author of sickness is Satan. God sent Jesus who took stripes upon His back for your healing:

> But he was wounded for our transgressions, he was bruised for our iniquities: the chastisement of our peace was upon him; and *with his stripes we are healed.*
> Isaiah 53:5 (KJV)

> Who his own self bare our sins in his own body on the tree, that we, being dead to sins, should live unto righteousness: *by whose stripes ye were healed.*
> 1 Peter 2:24 (KJV)

Many people say, "I'm not sure I can believe that." When this happens, a stronghold is exalting itself. It is standing up against the knowledge of God and trying to keep people from the experience of healing. The Bible is clear on this matter:

> Beloved, I wish above all things that thou mayest prosper and be in health, even as thy soul prospereth.
>
> 3 John 1:2 (KJV)

> Bless the LORD, O my soul, and forget not all his benefits:
> Who forgiveth all thine iniquities; who healeth all thy diseases.
>
> Psalm 103:2-3 (KJV)

God does not intend for you to be sick. That is a doctrine of devils. In the New Testament, God very clearly stated His doctrine for the Church:

> Is any one of you sick? *He should call the elders of the church to pray over him and anoint him with oil* in the name of the Lord.
> *And the prayer offered in faith will make the sick person well; the Lord will raise him up.* If he has sinned, he will be forgiven.
> Therefore confess your sins to each other and pray for each other so that you may be healed. The prayer of a righteous man is powerful and effective.
>
> James 5:14-16

Laying hands on the sick and anointing them with oil, coupled with the prayer of faith, is a biblical doctrine. Sickness is not.

Satan also will try to deceive you to believe that you can earn, merit, or deserve **salvation through works.** He wants you to think your salvation depends upon what you do or don't do. The Galatians in the Bible had fallen into this trap. They had begun to focus on works, instead of walking by faith according to grace. The Apostle Paul wrote one of his epistles to them precisely to correct this deception.

> ...Received ye the Spirit *by the works of the law, or by the hearing of faith?*
> Are ye so foolish? having begun in the Spirit, are ye now made perfect *by the flesh?*
>
> Galatians 3:2-3 (KJV)

Paul also wrote:

> *For by grace are ye saved* through faith; and that not of yourselves: it is the gift of God:
> *Not of works,* lest any man should boast.
>
> Ephesians 2:8-9 (KJV)

Another pet doctrine is that of **religious taboos** contrary to the Word of God. You must eliminate these activities of false humility, including self-imposed sufferings, fasts, and commands.

> Such regulations indeed have an appearance of wisdom, with their self-imposed worship, their false humility and their harsh treatment of the body, but they lack any value in restraining sensual indulgence.
>
> Colossians 2:23

It is critical for you to read the Word of God continually and stay in fellowship with Him. This is how you can recognize demonic doctrines. If a teaching or practice does not sound right, check it out according to the *entire* Bible, not just excerpts. A partial knowledge of the Word can lead to false conclusions. One way to know the proof of truth is to search the Bible from Genesis to Revelation. You can see the same scriptural truths over and over in the Word of God. His principles of truth span the entire text of the Bible.

Sexual Sins

Sexual immorality is one of the greatest strongholds in people's minds. The enemy successfully deceives many into committing sexual sins. Among other activities, these include homosexuality, incest, rape, adultery, prostitution, fornication, and promiscuity.

What is one of the mottoes in high schools today? "Whatever feels good, do it." Many believe the lie that says, "Sex is okay for us, because we 'love' each other."

However, sexual immorality is not confined to youth. Even nation's leaders fall to this debilitating sin, under the deception that certain kinds of acts do not constitute a sexual relationship. The devil enjoys publicity when he operates in the political world through the arrogance of men and women, who exalt themselves against the Word of God. Recently, we have seen dramatic proof of the devastation that sexual immorality can bring to an entire nation.

Sadly, this sin is not confined to unbelievers. Many in the Church—both adults and young people—fall prey to sexual sins. Even national Christian leaders are not exempt.

Why does the devil go to such great lengths to deceive people in this area? Satan knows that if he can tempt people to commit sexual sins, he can control them. Then, ultimately he can destroy them and those around them. Consider the following tragic results of sexual immorality, according to the Bible:

> Do you not know that the wicked will not inherit the kingdom of God? Do not be deceived: Neither the sexually immoral nor idolaters nor adulterers nor male prostitutes nor homosexual offenders nor thieves nor the greedy nor drunkards nor slanderers nor swindlers will inherit the kingdom of God.
>
> …The body is not meant for sexual immorality, but for the Lord, and the Lord for the body.
>
> Do you not know that your bodies are members of Christ himself? Shall I then take the members of Christ and unite them with a prostitute? Never!
>
> Do you not know that he who unites himself with a prostitute is one with her in body? For it is said, "The two will become one flesh."
>
> But he who unites himself with the Lord is one with him in spirit.
>
> Flee from sexual immorality. All other sins a man commits are outside his body, but he who sins sexually sins against his own body.
>
> Do you not know that your body is a temple of the Holy Spirit, who is in you, whom you have received from God? You are not your own;
>
> you were bought at a price. Therefore honor God with your body.
>
> 1 Corinthians 6:9-10, 13, 15-20

The King James Version states this last verse as follows:

> For ye are bought with a price: therefore glorify God

in your body, and in your spirit, which are God's.
1 Corinthians 6:20 (KJV)

The book of Proverbs contains many warnings about sexual sins:

For the lips of a strange woman drop as an honeycomb, and her mouth is smoother than oil:

But her end is bitter as wormwood, sharp as a two-edged sword.

Her feet go down to death; her steps take hold on hell.
Proverbs 5:3-5 (KJV)

For her [the adulteress'] house leads down to death and her paths to the spirits of the dead.

None who go to her return or attain the paths of life.
Proverbs 2:18-19

But whoso committeth adultery with a woman lacketh understanding: he that doeth it destroyeth his own soul.

A wound and dishonour shall he get; and his reproach shall not be wiped away.
Proverbs 6:32-33 (KJV)

In the book of Romans, Paul described the divine penalties for homosexuality:

Because of this, God gave them over to shameful lusts. Even their women exchanged natural relations for unnatural ones.

In the same way the men also abandoned natural

relations with women and were inflamed with lust for one another. Men committed indecent acts with other men, and received in themselves the due penalty for their perversion.

Furthermore, since they did not think it worthwhile to retain the knowledge of God, he gave them over to a depraved mind, to do what ought not to be done.

They have become filled with every kind of wickedness, evil, greed and depravity. They are full of envy, murder, strife, deceit and malice. They are gossips, slanderers, God-haters, insolent, arrogant and boastful; they invent ways of doing evil; they disobey their parents;

they are senseless, faithless, heartless, ruthless.

Although they know God's righteous decree that those who do such things deserve death, they not only continue to do these very things but also approve of those who practice them.

Romans 1:26-32

My heart grieves for those who engage in sexual sins. Many do not understand the disastrous results of this deception: Destruction.

Divorce

Demons also play a role in divorce. They deceive couples with the lie that divorce is an acceptable solution to their marital frustrations. However, the truth is that God forbids divorce (except in certain circumstances), and divorce does not completely solve couples' problems. Instead, divorce causes another set of troubles. Even when couples remarry their original spouses after divorcing, they have many difficulties to work through.

When Faye and I divorced, it took accurate and strategic spiritual warfare to restore our marriage. I know more people who have *not* won the conflict of separation and divorce than those who have. Why? It is because they lacked knowledge in the area of spiritual warfare and they believed the devil's lies.

When asked about divorce, Jesus described God's plan for marriage:

> Some Pharisees came and tested him by asking, "Is it lawful for a man to divorce his wife?"
>
> "What did Moses command you?" he replied.
>
> They said, "Moses permitted a man to write a certificate of divorce and send her away."
>
> "It was because your hearts were hard that Moses wrote you this law," Jesus replied.
>
> "But at the beginning of creation God 'made them male and female.'
>
> "'For this reason a man will leave his father and mother and be united to his wife,
>
> "'and the two will become one flesh.' *So they are no longer two, but one.*
>
> "*Therefore what God has joined together, let man not separate."*
>
> Mark 10:2-9

If your marriage is crumbling, this is not God's will, but the devil's. You see, if you do not understand what is happening and who is behind it, the devil can destroy your marriage. Contrary to popular belief, what you do not know *can* hurt you.

In fact, it can kill you and destroy everything that is important to you. Remember the verse in Hosea that we studied earlier:

> My people are destroyed for lack of knowledge....
> Hosea 4:6 (KJV)

A Christian husband and wife who obey God and walk in unity and agreement are a severe threat to the devil. That is why he tries so desperately to destroy marriages. Jesus said:

> Again I say unto you, That if two of you shall agree on earth as touching any thing that they shall ask, it shall be done for them of my Father which is in heaven.
> For where two or three are gathered together in my name, there am I in the midst of them.
> Matthew 18:19-20 (KJV)

As I mentioned in an earlier chapter, if you (or your friends and loved ones) need help in marriage, we have biblically based materials to help overcome the enemy in this area. Contact our ministry for more information. We have Bible School courses and several different tape series with study guides. Also, my book *It Only Takes One* will be of great help.

Do Not Fall for Deception

Do not ever forget that Satan's strategy is to lie and deceive you. Jesus said about the devil:

> ...He was a murderer from the beginning, not holding to the truth, for there is no truth in him. When he lies, he speaks his native language, for *he is a liar and the father of lies.*
> John 8:44

Have you ever said, "I can't," to God's direction, because the commitment cost more than you had? Instead of repeating the lies of the devil, you should declare the Words of the Bible:

> I can do all things through Christ which strengtheneth me.
>
> Philippians 4:13 (KJV)

Satan has come to drag you into deception. Do not listen to his lies, and definitely do not speak them forth!

> But I am afraid that just as Eve was deceived by the serpent's cunning, your minds may somehow be led astray from your sincere and pure devotion to Christ.
>
> 2 Corinthians 11:3

Break that deception, and walk in the light of God's truth!

16
Know How and
Why Demons Operate

As you study the Bible, you will find hundreds of accounts of Satan's demons in operation. Learning how to recognize demonic operation can help you to conquer your unseen enemies. You can cancel his assignments (such as sickness) in your life and in the lives of others. First, however, you must know that demons exist, and how and why they operate. The Scriptures contain these answers, which we will study in this chapter.

Jesus Delivered the Demon Possessed

In Jesus' lifetime on the earth, He saw the effects of Satan's activities in the people He met. How did He respond?

> While they were going out, a man who was demon-possessed and could not talk was brought to Jesus.
> And when the demon was driven out, the man who had been dumb spoke....
> Matthew 9:32-33

> Then they brought him a demon-possessed man who was blind and mute, and Jesus healed him, so that he could both talk and see.
> Matthew 12:22

These were not instances of physical healing, but of

deliverance from demons. Many physical afflictions are not issues of healing; they are issues of deliverance.

To operate effectively as ministers of God's power, we must identify where the enemy is operating. If not, we will pray for healing when an afflicted person really needs deliverance. Or we will try to cast demons off someone when demons are not the problem at all.

Deliverance from the Spirit of Blindness

Several yeas ago in Oklahoma, two other pastors and I went to a mental hospital to minister to a woman. She had nearly killed another woman. In retaliation, some of the injured woman's family members had beaten this mental patient severely. We went into the locked ward and sat down to visit her. The woman's face was contorted from the beating.

The two pastors began by witnessing to her. Soon, they led her to accept Jesus as her Savior. She was born-again, and a few minutes later she received the baptism in the Holy Spirit. Hallelujah!

Suddenly, the Holy Spirit showed me that an evil spirit had attached itself to the woman's eyes. We had not noticed any problems with her eyesight; and she had not mentioned anything wrong with her eyes. Yet, I knew there was a demon on her eyes. In Jesus' Name, I commanded it to come off her.

Then, I asked if she had a Bible, but she said she did not.

Upon opening and handing my Bible to her, I explained, "I want you to read 2 Timothy 1:7." She read the verse:

> For God hath not given us the spirit of fear; but of power, and of love, and of a sound mind.
>
> 2 Timothy 1:7 (KJV)

"I want you to confess that verse a hundred times," I instructed.

She read it and reread it. Then, she replied, "Okay, I will." As she stood up, I noticed that the attendant looked at her strangely.

That night, the woman's mother came to us at church and asked, "How's my daughter?"

"Oh, she's doing just great," I answered. "She became born-again and Spirit-filled!" Then I chided the mother a little: "Why haven't you ever given a Bible to your daughter?"

"Why would I give a Bible to her?" she asked.

"So she could read it!"

The woman looked puzzled. "No, my daughter is blind."

"Your daughter is *not* blind!" I insisted.

"What do you mean: She's 'not blind'? Didn't you see how the attendants had to take her by the arm wherever she went?"

Standing nearby was the woman's 12-year-old grand-daughter. This girl was the daughter of the battered woman in the hospital. I asked, "Was your mommy blind?"

"Oh, yes," she replied. "She had a little path that she walked in around the house. She knew exactly where she was going, but when she went to the store, I had to take her by the hand. She hasn't seen in years."

"Well," I responded, "she can see now! She is not blind anymore."

I looked at one of the pastors who had visited the woman with me. "Do you realize what happened? We never prayed for the healing of her eyes. We simply cast a spirit off her eyes, and she saw."

In reality, that woman's problem was not physical blindness. She did not have a natural condition that needed healing. Instead, an evil spirit had afflicted her eyes to the point that she could not see. When we cast that demon off her eyes, she saw clearly.

Deliverance from Deaf and Mute Spirits

I also have seen this happen with hundreds of deaf people. On numerous occasions, I have prayed for deaf people who needed re-creation in the inner ear, such as restoration of nerves or something similar. They needed *healing*.

However, some people to whom I have ministered had *deaf spirits*. They could not hear because spirits had attached themselves to these people's ears. Similarly, I have seen people who were mute. After I cast the evil spirits from them, they could articulate well.

Evil spirits can cause affliction and disease in our physical bodies.

Deliverance from the Spirit of Cancer

Once, in a meeting in Tulsa, Oklahoma, I was sitting in a service partaking of another minister's teaching. Suddenly, the Spirit of the Lord spoke to me, instructing me to cast a spirit of cancer off the woman who was sitting next to me! I was not scheduled to minister in this service, but God had another idea. This woman did not look sick. In fact, she did not even look as though she had a problem. However, I answered, "Well, Lord, I'll do it, if You say so."

The Lord commanded, "Yes, cast that spirit off her."

So I tapped her on the shoulder and politely asked, "I don't mean to be rude, but God just spoke to me. He told me that you have a spirit of cancer on you. When I asked Him further, He said that you have had several operations for cancer, but the doctors could not remove all of it. Is that true?"

"That's exactly right!" she responded.

"Well, it's not a physical problem we're dealing with," I explained. "It's an evil spirit. Will you let me take authority over that spirit?"

She was agreeable, so I took authority over it and cast it from her.

Later, after that time of ministry, the doctors performed biopsies on the woman. They checked every lymph node and all the previously afflicted areas. However, they could find nothing cancerous anywhere in the woman's entire body! Hallelujah!

Faye and I saw that same lady about two years later. She testified that she has had no further signs whatsoever of cancer in her body.

It was not simply cancer cells that caused that woman's disease. An evil spirit was moving from one part of her body to another, afflicting her. It was an evil spirit that had attached to her body.

You see, we must understand what evil spirits are and how they operate.

Jesus Delivered the Lunatic

Let's look at another case in Jesus' ministry:

> And when they were come to the multitude, there came to him a certain man, kneeling down to him, and saying,
>
> Lord, have mercy on my son: for he is a *lunatic*, and sore vexed: for ofttimes he falleth into the fire, and oft into the water.
>
> And I brought him to thy disciples, and they could not cure him.
>
> Matthew 17:14-16 (KJV)

An evil spirit controlled this man's son. The disciples did not know what to do with him. Most people did not know what to do with *me* before Pastor Hayden came, and the other pastors ministered deliverance to me! I thank God someone knew. People can act very crazy when evil spirits are working in their minds.

Let's continue the account of the man with the lunatic son. The books of Matthew and Mark both report this story. However, the King James Version of Matthew calls the spirit, "lunatic." Mark it names the demon, "deaf" and "dumb." We will refer to Mark for more detail about this boy:

> And when he [Jesus] came to his disciples, he saw a great multitude about them, and the scribes questioning with them.
> And straightway all the people, when they beheld him, were greatly amazed, and running to him saluted him.
> And he asked the scribes, What question ye with them?
> And one of the multitude answered and said, Master, I have brought unto thee my son, which hath a *dumb spirit*.
> Mark 9:14-17 (KJV)

This next passage clarifies what a lunatic spirit is. You might not realize that a "dumb spirit" also would cause a person to be a lunatic. However, it did far more than merely rob him of speech. Let's continue this account:

> "Whenever it seizes him, it throws him to the ground. He foams at the mouth, gnashes his teeth and becomes rigid. I asked your disciples to drive out the spirit, but they could not."
> "O unbelieving generation," Jesus replied, "how

long shall I stay with you? How long shall I put up with you? Bring the boy to me."

So they brought him. When the spirit saw Jesus, it immediately threw the boy into a convulsion. He fell to the ground and rolled around, foaming at the mouth.

Jesus asked the boy's father, "How long has he been like this?"

"From childhood," he answered. "It has often thrown him into fire or water to kill him. But if you can do anything, take pity on us and help us."

"'If you can'?" said Jesus. "Everything is possible for him who believes."

Immediately the boy's father exclaimed, "I do believe; help me overcome my unbelief!"

When Jesus saw that a crowd was running to the scene, he rebuked the evil spirit. "You deaf and dumb spirit," he said, "I command you, come out of him and never enter him again."

The spirit shrieked, convulsed him violently and came out. The boy looked so much like a corpse that many said, "He's dead."

But Jesus took him by the hand and lifted him to his feet, and he stood up.

Mark 9:18-27

Later, when the disciples asked Jesus why they could not cast out this spirit:

He [Jesus] replied, "This kind can come out only by prayer [some manuscripts add *and fasting*]."

Mark 9:29

God's Chosen Fast

Sometimes, when ministering to the demon-oppressed, we must spend extra time before the Lord. It might take a commitment to fast and pray. However, most of the time, we do not have to do this. Only a few times has the Holy Spirit directed me to fast and pray before deliverance. Mostly, God sets people free when I simply obey His Holy Spirit and speak in the Name of Jesus.

For those cases in which God calls you to fast, remember the purpose of fasting:

> Is not this the fast that I have chosen? to loose the bands of wickedness, to undo the heavy burdens, and to let the oppressed go free, and that ye break every yoke?
> Isaiah 58:6 (KJV)

Here God explained the powerful results you can expect when He calls you to fast. His power will:

- Loose the bands of wickedness.
- Undo the heavy burdens.
- Let the oppressed go free.
- Break every yoke.

Jesus Delivered the Demoniac from the Gadarenes

Now, let's read about how Jesus delivered the demoniac from the Gadarenes (KJV) or Gerasenes (NIV):

> They sailed to the region of the Gerasenes, which is across the lake from Galilee.
> When Jesus stepped ashore, he was met by a demon-

possessed man from the town. For a long time this man *had not worn clothes* or lived in a house, but had *lived in the tombs.*

When he saw Jesus, he cried out and fell at his feet, shouting at the top of his voice, "What do you want with me, Jesus, Son of the Most High God? I beg you, don't torture me!"

For Jesus had commanded the evil spirit to come out of the man. Many times it had seized him, and though he was chained hand and foot and kept under guard, *he had broken his chains* and had been *driven by the demon into solitary places.*

Jesus asked him, "What is your name?" "Legion," he replied, because many demons had gone into him.

And they begged him repeatedly not to order them to go into the Abyss.

A large herd of pigs was feeding there on the hillside. The demons begged Jesus to let them go into them, and he gave them permission.

When the demons came out of the man, they went into the pigs, and the herd rushed down the steep bank into the lake and was drowned.

When those tending the pigs saw what had happened, they ran off and reported this in the town and countryside,

and the people went out to see what had happened. When they came to Jesus, they found the man from whom the demons had gone out, sitting at Jesus' feet, dressed and in his right mind; and they were afraid.

Those who had seen it told the people how the demon-possessed man had been cured.

Then all the people of the region of the Gerasenes asked Jesus to leave them, because they were overcome with fear. So he got into the boat and left.

The man from whom the demons had gone out begged to go with him, but Jesus sent him away, saying,

"Return home and tell how much God has done for you." So the man went away and told all over town how much Jesus had done for him.

Luke 8:26-39

Mark's account records more detail of this demoniac's behavior:

They went across the lake to the region of the Gerasenes.

When Jesus got out of the boat, a man with an evil spirit came from the tombs to meet him.

This man lived in the tombs, and no one could bind him any more, not even with a chain.

For he had often been chained hand and foot, but he tore the chains apart and broke the irons on his feet. No one was strong enough to subdue him.

Night and day among the tombs and in the hills he would cry out and cut himself with stones.

Mark 5:1-5

Manifestations of Demonic Activity

When evil spirits are at work in a person, they can exhibit frightening and bizarre behaviors. Included in the above account are several examples.

Insanity. Often, demons cause insanity, which usually results in bizarre behavior. Here, the insanity of the man from the Gadarenes caused him to live "in the tombs" and "solitary places." Then, "night and day among the tombs and in the hills he would cry out." Before my deliverance, I was insane from demonic activity and often cried out.

Cutting or mutilating oneself. Taking sharp stones and trying to cut or kill oneself is common demonic activity, as illustrated here. Slitting one's wrist is nothing new to humanity. Have you ever heard of someone cutting himself with razor blades, trying to commit suicide? This and other attempts as self-destruction or suicide are forms of demonic activity. I also experienced this before my deliverance.

Extra physical strength. Not even iron chains could hold this demon-possessed man from the Gadarenes! Faye and I have seen it take several men to hold people down for deliverance. For example, we have seen a frail, little woman with enough strength that it took five men to hold her down during deliverance!

One very effective strategy to stop such strength is to command it: "I bind you, spirit, from manifesting in Jesus' Name, now!" We will discuss this further in a later chapter.

Nakedness. Before his deliverance, the man from the Gadarenes wore no clothes in public. In Indonesia, there was a woman who ran around naked the entire time we were there. She would not wear clothes, nor would she live in a house. This sounds like the man we just read about in the Bible. Yes, demons can get hold of people and make them act very strangely.

Go to the Oppressed

In some Third World countries, such people freely walk around in the streets. There, Christians can minister to them openly. However, in America, usually we must obtain permission to go into hospitals to minister to these kinds of tormented people.

Follow the example of Jesus as He obeyed His Father:

> Then answered Jesus and said unto them, Verily, verily, I say unto you, The Son can do nothing of himself, but what he seeth the Father do: for what things soever he doeth, these also doeth the Son likewise.
>
> John 5:19 (KJV)

We must hear, see, and do what Jesus, our Example, did! What did He do?

> How God anointed Jesus of Nazareth with the Holy Ghost and with power: who went about doing good, and healing all that were oppressed of the devil; for God was with him.
>
> Acts 10:38 (KJV)

Follow Him, and you will destroy the deeds of darkness in His Name! The Lord promises that you can conquer your unseen enemies.

> That ye be not slothful, but followers of them who through faith and patience inherit the promises.
>
> Hebrews 6:12 (KJV)

17
Bind and Loose

The Spirit of God inspired the writers of the Bible to describe our position in Jesus Christ as one of authority, dominion, and power. We have learned that the Holy Spirit empowers us and reveals spiritual matters to our human spirits, so we can identify and locate the enemy's operations. The only part left is to act! Become proactive to get rid of him! In this chapter, we will discuss how to do that.

Confront Boldly with Authority

Picture a demon as a little dog. Let's say, for example, a man is walking down the street, and a dog begins nipping at his heels. As he walks, the man calmly says to the pest, "Get away from me. You bother me."

However, the dog continues to pester him. Irritated, the man instructs with a slightly stronger voice, "I said, dog, to leave me alone." The dog backs off a little; but soon comes back, biting at the man's heels, again.

Finally, the man thinks, *I've had it. I'm tired of this dog coming after me. I will not put up with it anymore.* He stops, turns to the dog, and boldly commands, "Now, *git!*" The dog runs away, because of the authority and commanding voice!

Likewise, many Christians politely say: "Satan, just leave me alone, today. Okay? I want to have a good day." The devil does not respond to this kind of language. You cannot reason with him. He is like that small dog. He might back off a little at first. However, he will continue to come back, unless you confront him boldly with authority in Jesus' Name.

The Apostle Paul wrote to the Christians at Ephesus regarding God's purpose for his life:

> And *to make all men see* what is the fellowship of the mystery, which from the beginning of the world hath been hid in God, who created all things by Jesus Christ:
>
> To the intent that now unto *the principalities and powers [demons] in heavenly places might be known by the church the manifold wisdom of God,*
>
> According to the eternal purpose which he purposed in Christ Jesus our Lord:
>
> In whom we have boldness and access with confidence by the faith of him.
>
> Ephesians 3:9-12 (KJV)

God has called Paul and all Christians after him to make the wisdom of God plain to mankind, the devil, and his demons. We must be clear, bold, and authoritative when we speak.

Like that dog, the devil and his demons understand authority. They recognize when you have absolute conviction and resolve in a matter. If you even slightly waver, they may come back to hinder you. Remember:

> Neither give place to the devil.
>
> Ephesians 4:27 (KJV)

Demons know what the Word of God says about wavering:

> If any of you lack wisdom, let him ask of God, that

giveth to all men liberally, and upbraideth not; and it shall be given him.

But let him ask in faith, nothing wavering. For he that wavereth is like a wave of the sea driven with the wind and tossed.

For let not that man think that he shall receive any thing of the Lord.

A double minded man is unstable in all his ways.

James 1:5-8 (KJV)

Attack the Gates of Hell

As recorded in the book of Matthew, Jesus said:

And I say also unto thee, That thou art Peter, and upon this rock *I will build my church; and the gates of hell shall not prevail against it.*

Matthew 16:18 (KJV)

Many have interpreted this verse to mean that the enemy will not prevail over the Church because Jesus is our Defense. While this is a true statement, I question that interpretation, here. Have you ever seen a gate attack anyone? No. Why? Gates are not offensive weapons. The gates of Hell do not *attack the Church;* they *defend Hell.* We do not need to run from the gates of Hell; they are not attacking us. No, the Church is to attack and break through the gates of Hell!

The way we do this is to free the people who are on the way to Hell—under the enemy's deceit and control—in Jesus' Name! At every juncture of life, God has called us to set at liberty those who are bound, to open blind eyes, to heal the sick, and to cast out demons. Our position is absolute dominion, and the proof of our victory is the power of Jesus' Name.

You see, the forces of the enemy have bound humans in every area including their bodies, minds, families, finances, social lives, and governments. These demonic forces have kept people from knowing the truth of God's Word, by exalting themselves against the knowledge of God. Today, God is calling you and me to release people from these spiritual forces. We are liberators—ones who set others free.

Get ready! As soon as you personally experience *your* freedom, God requires you to liberate others. Remember, Jesus commanded:

> ...Go ye into all the world, and preach the gospel to every creature.
> He that believeth and is baptized shall be saved; but he that believeth not shall be damned.
> And these signs shall follow them that believe; In my name shall they cast out devils; they shall speak with new tongues;
> They shall take up serpents; and if they drink any deadly thing, it shall not hurt them; they shall lay hands on the sick, and they shall recover.
> Mark 16:15-18 (KJV)

Bind the Spirits

Instead of allowing the spirits to bind people, the Church is to bind the demons, and then set the people free.

Jesus said that He will give to us the keys of the Kingdom of Heaven and the ability to bind and loose:

> "I will give you the keys of the kingdom of heaven;

whatever you bind on earth will be bound in heaven, *and whatever you loose on earth will be loosed in heaven."*

Matthew 16:19

Whatever we loose on earth shall be loosed in the heavenlies, where the demonic spirit realms operate.

Similarly, Jesus said:

Verily I say unto you, Whatsoever ye shall bind on earth shall be bound in heaven: and whatsoever ye shall loose on earth shall be loosed in heaven.

Matthew 18:18 (KJV)

Let's examine other passages in the Bible concern binding. Regarding "the saints," the psalmist wrote:

Let the high praises of God be in their mouth, and a two-edged sword in their hand;

To execute vengeance upon the heathen, and punishments upon the people;

To bind their kings with chains, and their nobles with fetters of iron;

To execute upon them the judgment written: this honour have all his saints. Praise ye the LORD.

Psalm 149:6-9 (KJV)

These verses describe God's mandate for the Israelites to carry out His judgment against His Old Testament enemies.

However, as we studied earlier, the warfare for New Testament believers is no longer against flesh and blood. Instead of a "two-edged sword" in our hands for physical wars,

New Testament believers have a better weapon for our spiritual battles:

> For the word of God is living and active. *Sharper than any double-edged sword,* it penetrates even to dividing soul and spirit, joints and marrow; it judges the thoughts and attitudes of the heart.
>
> Hebrews 4:12

Today, we use the Word of God and other spiritual weapons to bind the spiritual demonic kings and nobles. This is how we "execute upon them the judgment written." Hallelujah! God has chosen YOU and me to conquer His unseen spiritual enemies—to walk in His power and victory!

As recorded in the book of Mark, Jesus said:

> No man can enter into a strong man's house, and spoil his goods, except he will *first bind the strong man;* and then he will spoil his house.
>
> Mark 3:27 (KJV)

When recognizing a demonic problem, we must "first bind the strong man," the primary spirit that has attached itself to the person and is causing the major problem.

Today, the spoken word binds the enemy. Simply command the demon, "I bind you in the Name of Jesus." By saying this, you restrain the spirit's ability to operate. You restrict its behavior. When you limit a demon's activity, the deliverance is far less violent and showy. Demons like to flaunt themselves and make big productions during deliverance.

Whenever you deal with a demon, I highly recommend that you first bind it in the Name of Jesus. Do not allow a spirit to speak or to manifest itself. You have authority over whether it manifests. If the demon starts to act up, or the person looks or sounds strange, you can stop it. Command the spirit: "I bind you from manifesting in Jesus' Name."

Once, when I was ministering in a church in Tulsa, Oklahoma, a man said he needed prayer. We walked into a tiny room on the side of the platform and started to pray. Suddenly, he informed me that he was about to vomit. Since I was the only person in the room praying for him, I would be a likely target for this demonic display! "No, you're not!" I quickly ordered the spirit. "In the Name of Jesus of Nazareth, I bind you from manifesting!"

"Oh," the man said, " I feel better!"

"I know you do," I replied.

You do not have to endure demonic activities during deliverance. Do not allow the devil put on a show. It is that simple. Give him no place.

Command the Spirit to Come Out

After you bind the spirit—and bind it from manifesting, if necessary—then, command it to come out in the Name of Jesus. This is not requesting. It is not asking, "Oh, demons, would you mind stepping aside?" They always mind stepping aside. No, you *command* them to leave in Jesus' Name.

Remember, in Acts 16:18, when dealing with the slave girl, who had a spirit of fortunetelling, Paul simply said to the demon:

> …I command thee in the name of Jesus Christ to come out of her. And he came out the same hour.
>
> Acts 16:18 (KJV)

This is how you must treat demons. Remember:

The weapons we fight with are not the weapons of the world. On the contrary, they have divine power *to demolish strongholds.*

We demolish arguments and every pretension that sets itself up against the knowledge of God, and we take captive every thought to make it obedient to Christ.

2 Corinthians 10:4-5

You have strong spiritual weapons to demolish the devil's strongholds. Exercise your authority in Jesus' Name, not knowledge or arguments. Simply speak with authority. It does not need to be loud. Demons hear authority, not volume.

Sometimes, we need to be spiritually violent with demons.

And from the days of John the Baptist until now *the kingdom of heaven suffereth violence, and the violent take it by force.*

Matthew 11:12 (KJV)

When I pray with someone, the enemy knows that I will become violent in my prayer, if he manifests. I will become angry with him and stop his show in Jesus' Name. I cannot afford for the enemy to repeat what he did to me in the past. I have been there once, and I will not let him lay a finger on me, again.

This Is War!

Remember, the thief comes to rob, kill, and destroy. He is not playing games with us. No! He wants to kill us, break up our families, rob our finances, and give diseases to us. This is war, my friend! We engage in spiritual battles. What we know will cause us to win. What we *do not* know will cause us to lose. The stakes are very high. We must know who we are in Christ, know what to do, and do it. We have the souls in the whole world to gain for the glory of God!

Do Your Part, and God Will Do His

I encourage you to be faithful in doing your part in conquering your unseen enemies. As you do, God will perform His Word with signs following. Trust in and rely upon Him—not yourself—and you will see great victories!

> ...We have heard with our ears, O God, our fathers have told us, what work thou didst in their days, in the times of old.
>
> How thou didst drive out the heathen with thy hand, and plantedst them; how thou didst afflict the people, and cast them out.
>
> For they got not the land in possession by their own sword, neither did their own arm save them: but thy right hand, and thine arm, and the light of thy countenance, because thou hadst a favour unto them.
>
> Thou art my King, O God: command deliverances for Jacob.
>
> Through thee will we push down our enemies: through thy name will we tread them under that rise up against us.
>
> For I will not trust in my bow, neither shall my sword save me.
>
> But thou hast saved us from our enemies, and hast put them to shame that hated us.
>
> In God we boast all the day long, and praise thy name for ever. Selah.
>
> Psalm 44:1-8 (KJV)

Do not ever quit until you have won. Be sure that you know God's Word. Take authority and command the devil. See yourself dead to sin and alive in Christ. Recognize that you do not have that old sin nature. You have a new-creation nature of righteousness. Live in the victory and triumph that Jesus has given to you!

Then, regardless of the circumstances, do not surrender your victory, and be vigilant. Remember, Jesus warned:

> "When an evil spirit comes out of a man, it goes through arid places seeking rest and does not find it.
>
> "Then it says, 'I will return to the house I left.' When it arrives, it finds the house unoccupied, swept clean and put in order.
>
> "Then it goes and takes with it seven other spirits more wicked than itself, and they go in and live there. And the final condition of that man is worse than the first. That is how it will be with this wicked generation."
>
> Matthew 12:43-45

To maintain your freedom, I encourage you to:

- Become filled with the Holy Spirit. (See Appendix.) Pray in tongues often.
- Stay in the Word of God and fellowship with Him daily.
- Find a biblical leader, such as a local pastor, to learn from regularly.
- Make new Christian friends.

Now, go conquer your unseen enemies in Jesus' Name!

Part 4

Handbook

for

Spiritual Warfare

Contents

On the following pages,
you will find information
and Scripture references
to help you
conquer your unseen enemies
in spiritual warfare.

Glossary

Authority

Matthew 28:18—lawful right in the sense of ability; delegated influences; jurisdiction; power with the legal right to use it.

Bound or bind

Matthew 16:19—any sort of binding; to hold or restrain.

Demons or devils

Luke 11:20—supernatural spirits (of a bad nature); from the root word *to know*—thus, "knowing beings."

Destroy

1 John 3:8—to render powerless; to loosen; to loose; render free.

Romans 6:6 (*the body of sin destroyed*)—to render entirely useless; to bring to naught; vanish away; make void.

John 10:10—destroy to the full; to mar; die.

High thing

2 Corinthians 10:5—an elevated place or thing, spiritual barrier.

Idol

Acts 7:41—an object that attracts the power of demons. Demons work through idols. They are the spiritual agents in all idolatry. The idol is nothing, but the demon induces idolatry with its worship and sacrifices. An idol draws adoration. It can be anything that assists worship.

Imaginations

2 Corinthians 10:5—reasonings.

Know

Romans 6:6—absolutely know; to know intimately.

Romans 6:9—to know; behold; be aware.

Loose

Matthew 16:19—to unbind, release, to put off, to set free, to discharge from prison.

Power

Acts 1:8—force, miraculous power; ability; strength; mighty (wonderful) work.

Powers

Ephesians 6:12—authorities (Greek: *exousia*).

Principalities

Ephesians 6:12—used to describe territories ruled by a prince, ruler, magistrate, or leader.

Sin or Sin Nature

Romans 6:7—the spiritual nature in the unbeliever that induces one habitually and continually to commit acts of wrongdoing.

Sins

1 John 1:9—the acts of wrongdoing.

Spiritual wickedness [in high places]

Ephesians 6:12—huge numbers of wicked spirits in the spirit world.

Strongholds

2 Corinthians 10:4—to fortify through the idea of holding safely; arguments.

Thrones

Colossians 1:16—holders of dominion or authority; power or rank of a king; an order of angels.

World rulers

Ephesians 6:12—lords of this world; princes of this age.

Facts about Demons

You must know the unseen enemies that face you.

Demons Name Themselves

Very often evil spirits will name themselves. This is not always the case; nor is it always necessary to know the name of a demon to cast it out. However, we do need to know the area of demonic involvement. Remember that demons are *liars* and may not tell the truth about their names, numbers, or strength (John 8:44).

What Demons Are and Are Not

Demons are angels who fell from Heaven with Lucifer when he sinned. They are not the spirits of dead people or the offspring of angels and men.

Where Do Demons Dwell?

Demons dwell in the earth and its atmosphere (Ephesians 2:1-2). They are not in Hell, yet. However, they do have an appointed time of judgment (Matthew 8:29). Demons on earth in Christ's time still inhabit bodies of persons today.

What Will Become of Demons?

The devil and his angels will be bound and cast into the bottomless pit (Revelation 20:1-10, KJV).

Demons Believe and Tremble

"Thou believest that there is one God; thou doest well: the

devils also believe, and tremble" (James 2:19, KJV).

Demons Have Willpower

"You [Lucifer] said in your heart, 'I *will* ascend to heaven; I *will* raise my throne above the stars of God; I *will* sit enthroned on the mount of assembly, on the utmost heights of the sacred mountain. I *will* ascend above the tops of the clouds; I *will* make myself like the Most High'" (Isaiah 14:13-14).

"Then it [demon] says, 'I *will* return to the house I left.' When it arrives, it finds the house unoccupied, swept clean and put in order" (Matthew 12:44).

Demons Have Doctrines

"The Spirit clearly says that in later times some will abandon the faith and follow deceiving spirits and things taught by demons" (1 Timothy 4:1).

Demons Are Subject to Christ

"[Jesus Christ] Who is gone into heaven, and is on the right hand of God; angels and authorities and powers being made subject unto him" (1 Peter 3:22, KJV).

Demons Oppose Saints of God

"For I am convinced that...neither angels nor demons...nor any powers...will be able to separate us from the love of God that is in Christ Jesus our Lord" (Romans 8:38-39).

"...He [the devil] was a murderer from the beginning, not holding to the truth, for there is no truth in him. When he lies, he speaks his native language, for he is a liar and the father of lies" (John 8:44).

Demonic Activity

Astrology	Deuteronomy 17:3
Blindness and dumbness	Matthew 12:22
Body sores	Job 2:7
Bondage	Romans 8:15
Cities of devil's dominion	Revelation 2:13
Confusion	James 3:16
Convulsions	Luke 4:35
Covetousness, greed	Colossians 3:5; 1 Timothy 6:10
Deaf and dumb	Mark 9:25; Matthew 9:32-34
Divinations	Acts 16:16
Doctrines of demons	1 Timothy 4:1
Envy	James 3:14-16
Evil spirits	Judges 9:23; Luke 7:21
Fear	2 Timothy 1:7
Fear of death	Hebrews 2:14-15
Familiar spirits	Deuteronomy 18:9-12; 1 Samuel 28:7; 2 Kings 21:6; 1 Chronicles 10:13; 2 Chronicles 33:6
Harm	Matthew 17:15; Luke 8:27-39
Heaviness (depression)	Isaiah 61:3
Infirmity	Luke 13:11-12
Jealousy	Numbers 5:11-31
Kill	John 10:10

Lunatic	Matthew 17:14-21
Lying	1 Kings 22:21-23; Acts 5:3; John 8:44
Nakedness	Luke 8:27
Rebellion	1 Samuel 15:23
Seducing	1 Timothy 4:1
Spirit spoke	Matthew 8:31; Luke 4:33-34; Acts 19:15-16
Strife	James 3:14-16
Tempter	Matthew 4:3
Thief	John 10:10
Unclean spirits	Zechariah 13:2; Matthew 12:43-45; Mark 1:23-27, 3:11, 5:2-15, 6:7-13, 7:25-30; Luke 4:33-36, 6:18, 8:29, 9:42
Whoredoms	Hosea 4:12, 5:4
World of politics	Daniel 10:13, 20

Occult Objects, Groups, Practices, and Beliefs

Allhallows Eve

> The day witches celebrate above all others, October 31. Considered by witches to be a sacred, deadly, and powerful time; a pagan belief.

Amulet

> An ornament or gem worn on the body as protection against evil spirits.

Animism

> A widely held belief—especially in Central Africa, parts of Asia, and some Pacific Islands—that souls are quasi-physical and can exist outside the body (in dreams and visions); can be transferred from one body to another; and persist after death of the body.

Astral projection

> The belief that a person can will his soul to leave his body and travel at will to any place in the world or universe. It is said that a "silver cord" keeps the body alive by providing the individual return access. Some fear the danger of the cord being cut or that another spirit would inhabit the unattended body.

Astrology

> The art of predicting or determining the influence of the planets and stars on human affairs.

Augury

> The practice of divination from omens.

Automatic writing
Writing performed without conscious intention and sometimes without awareness, as if of telepathic or spiritual origin.

Bewitch
To fascinate or charm; to affect by witchcraft.

Black mass
A travesty of the Christian mass in devil worship.

Cartomancy
Fortunetelling by cards.

Charm
An incantation, especially as a protection against evil or danger; a formula or action supposed to have a supernatural power against evil.

Chiromancy
Palmistry, the practice of divining a person's character and future by studying the palm of his hand.

Clairvoyance
A second sight; use of a medium who forecasts distant happenings through visions; ability to know instantly things about people, places, or events that were not previously known by the individual through natural means.

Clairvoyant
Having second sight; someone who has clairvoyance.

Conjure up
To bring vividly before the imagination as though by magic; to summon up (a spirit) by invocation.

Coven
An assembly of thirteen witches.

Crystal gazer
A person who practices the art of concentrating on a glass or

crystal ball with the aim of inducing a psychic state in which divination can be performed; the attempt to predict future events or make difficult judgments, especially without adequate data.

Cult

An unorthodox system of religious worship; a sect; extravagant admiration of or devotion to a person, principle, or thing.

Curse

An invocation or prayer for harm or divine punishment to come upon someone.

Demon

An evil spirit; a wicked, destructive creature; an evil attendant power or spirit subservient to Satan.

Divination

A foretelling of the future or the unknown by supernatural means.

Dream incubation

The ritual of sleeping in a sacred place in hopes of receiving a divinely inspired dream; recognized by several ancient cultures as a means of guidance and healing.

Enchanter

A magician.

Enchantment

A magic spell or charm; the state of being under a spell.

Esbat

A meeting of witches held for the transacting of business or to accomplish an act of satanic mischief.

Exorcise

To drive out or ward off an evil spirit.

Exorcism

The act or process of driving out evil spirits, commanding

them in the name of God to depart, or by using charms, incantations, etc., to free a person or place from the possession of evil spirits.

Extrasensory

Outside the senses; involving a source other than the senses; as in *extrasensory perception* or *ESP*.

Familiar spirit

A demon who comes at the call of a witch or wizard; a demon who has knowledge of the present or future.

Fetish

An object believed to embody a spirit and exert magical powers.

Fortuneteller

A person who claims to foretell the future and makes money from the claim.

Graphology

The study of handwriting and the inferring of character or aptitude from it.

Hex

An evil spell; to put an evil spell on; to bewitch.

Horoscope

The configuration of the planets, especially at the time of a person's birth, from which astrologers predict his future.

Incantation

A use of spells or verbal charms spoken or sung as a part of a ritual of magic; a formula of words used in or as if in such a ritual.

Invocation

A formula for conjuring; an incantation.

Levitation

The act or process of levitating, especially the rising of a person or thing by means held to be supernatural.

Magic

The art, which claims to control and manipulate the secret forces of nature by occult and ritualistic methods. **Black magic:** magic used in the service of evil. **White magic:** use of witchcraft for good. [Note: These are dictionary definitions. Those practicing either black or white magic use occult methods to accomplish *their own purposes.*]

Meditation

To reflect deeply; to spend time in the spiritual exercise of thinking about some religious theme; deep, serious thought; reflection on a religious subject as a spiritual exercise as in *transcendental meditation* or *TM.*

Medium

A person credited with special powers for communicating between the living and the dead.

Mystic

A person who believes in mysticism, has mystical experiences, or follows a mystical way of life.

Mysticism

A doctrine or belief that direct spiritual apprehension of truth or union with God may be obtained through contemplation or insight in ways inaccessible to the senses or reason.

Necromancy

Conjuration of the spirits of the dead for the purposes of magically revealing the future or influencing the course of events.

Observers of time

Astrologers.

Occult

Beyond the range of normal perception; secret; mysterious;

esoteric; dealing with magic and astrology.

Omen

An event or phenomenon believed to be a sign or warning of a future occurrence.

Ouija board

A board marked with the alphabet and various signs, fitted with a planchette and used to obtain messages in spiritualist practice.

Palmistry

The practice or profession of foretelling a person's future or reading his character by interpreting the crease lines in the palm and other aspects of the hand.

Planchette

A small, heart-shaped board supported by two castors and a pencil or stylus, which, when moved across the surface by the light, unguided pressure of the finger tips, is supposed to trace meaningful patterns or written messages revealing subconscious thoughts, psychic phenomena, clairvoyant messages, etc.

Poltergeist

A mischievous spirit, which manifests its presence by throwing objects about noisily.

Potions

Doses of medicine, poison, or drugs in liquid form used to bring spiritual blessing or cursing upon an individual.

Psychic phenomena

Events, which cannot be explained by physical reference and are attributed to spiritual forces.

Psychokinesis

Mind over matter; ability to have physical influence over matter (apart from one's own body) through the use of visualization or thought.

Psychometry

Divination of facts concerning an object or its owner through contact with or proximity to the object.

Reincarnation

Rebirth of a human soul into a new human body.

Rhabdomancy

Divination by means of a wand or stick.

Sabbat

Main meeting of witches to bring in new members.

Satanic church

Refers to any group practicing Satanism.

Satanism

Worship of Satan using rites, which are travesties of Christian rites.

Seance

Meeting in which spiritualists profess to communicate with the dead.

Soothsaying

Predicting the future.

Sorcerer

A person who practices sorcery; a wizard or witch.

Sorcery

The use of magic; witchcraft.

Spell

A magic formula; incantation; a controlling influence.

Spiritism

The belief that natural objects have indwelling spirits.

Spiritualism

The doctrine that the spirit, surviving after the death of the body, can communicate with persons still living.

Talisman

An object, especially a figure carved or cut at a time considered astrologically favorable, which is supposed to have magical protective qualities.

Tarot

One of a set of playing cards first used in Italy in the 14th century. The figured cards are used in fortunetelling and as trumps in the game played with the entire set.

Telepathy

Apparent communication from one mind to another by extrasensory means.

Transmigration

Rebirth of any soul into a different life form.

Voodoo

An Animist religion accompanied by black magic. It was originally African and is still practiced by some cultures in the West Indies.

Witch

A woman practicing sorcery, usually with the aid of or through the medium of an evil spirit.

Wizard

A sorcerer, magician; a person who seems to perform magic.

Your Authority

And the seventy returned again with joy, saying,
Lord, even the devils are subject unto us through thy name.

Luke 10:17 (KJV)

I. **New Creation Man—by the Blood**
   "And they overcame him [Satan] by the blood of the
   Lamb [Jesus], and by the word of their testimony; and
   they loved not their lives unto the death" (Revelation
   12:11, KJV).

A. *Firstborn of every creature.* "[Jesus] Who is the image of
   the invisible God, the firstborn of every creature: For by
   him were all things created, that are in heaven, and that
   are in earth, visible and invisible, whether they be thrones,
   or dominions, or principalities, or powers: all things
   were created by him, and for him: And he is before all
   things, and by him all things consist. And he is the head
   of the body, the church: who is the beginning, the firstborn
   from the dead; that in all things he might have the
   preeminence" (Colossians 1:15-18, KJV).

B. *Firstborn among many brothers.* "For those God foreknew
   he also predestined to be conformed to the likeness of his
   Son, that he might be the firstborn among many brothers"
   (Romans 8:29).

C. *Brothers to Jesus.* "Both the one who makes men holy and those who are made holy are of the same family. So Jesus is not ashamed to call them brothers" (Hebrews 2:11).

D. *New birth through resurrection.* "Praise be to the God and Father of our Lord Jesus Christ! In his great mercy he has given us new birth into a living hope through the resurrection of Jesus Christ from the dead" (1 Peter 1:3).

E. *A new creation.* "Therefore, if anyone is in Christ, he is a new creation; the old has gone, the new has come" (2 Corinthians 5:17).

II. We Are in Him with Power through Him

A. *In Him at the right hand of the Father.*
   1. Raised together. "And God raised us up with Christ and seated us with him in the heavenly realms in Christ Jesus" (Ephesians 2:6).
   2. Delivered. "For he has rescued [delivered] us from the dominion of darkness and brought us into the kingdom of the Son he loves" (Colossians 1:13).
   3. Hidden. "For ye are dead, and your life is hid with Christ in God" (Colossians 3:3, KJV).

B. *Power through God.*
   1. Divine power. "The weapons we fight with are not the weapons of the world. On the contrary, they have divine power to demolish strongholds" (2 Corinthians 10:4).

2. Mighty power. "Finally, be strong in the Lord and in his mighty power" (Ephesians 6:10).
3. More than conquerors. "Nay, in all these things we are more than conquerors through him that loved us" (Romans 8:37, KJV).

III. We Have the Spirit of God in Power

A. *Power.* "But ye shall receive power, after that the Holy Ghost is come upon you: and ye shall be witnesses unto me both in Jerusalem, and in all Judaea, and in Samaria, and unto the uttermost part of the earth" (Acts 1:8, KJV).

B. *Greater power in you.* "You, dear children, are from God and have overcome them, because the one who is in you is greater than the one who is in the world" (1 John 4:4).

C. *God's Spirit.* "The Spirit of the Lord is upon me, because he hath anointed me to preach the gospel to the poor; he hath sent me to heal the brokenhearted, to preach deliverance to the captives, and recovering of sight to the blind, to set at liberty them that are bruised" (Luke 4:18, KJV).

D. *Yoke destroyed.* "…The yoke shall be destroyed because of the anointing" (Isaiah 10:27, KJV).

E. *Drive out demons.* "But if I drive out demons by the Spirit of God, then the kingdom of God has come upon you" (Matthew 12:28).

IV. Direct Command from Jesus to Have Power and Authority

A. *He gives power and authority.* "Then he called his twelve disciples together, and gave them power and authority over all devils, and to cure diseases" (Luke 9:1, KJV). "And these signs will accompany those who believe: In my name they will drive out demons; they will speak in new tongues" (Mark 16:17).

B. *He gives authority over the enemy.* "Behold, I give unto you power...over all the power of the enemy: and nothing shall by any means hurt you" (Luke 10:19, KJV).

V. We Have Spiritual Armor

A. *Armor of light.* "...So let us put aside the deeds of darkness and put on the armor of light" (Romans 13:12).

B. *Armor of righteousness.* "By the word of truth, by the power of God, by the armor of righteousness on the right hand and the left" (2 Corinthians 6:7, KJV).

C. *Armor of God.* "Put on the full armor of God so that you can take your stand against the devil's schemes. For our struggle is not against flesh and blood, but against the rulers, against the authorities, against the powers of this dark world and against the spiritual forces of evil in the heavenly realms. Therefore put on the full armor of God, so that when the day of evil comes, you may be able to stand your ground, and after you have done everything, to stand" (Ephesians 6:11-13).

VI.   We Have the Name of Jesus

A. *Jesus gives us "power of attorney."*

B. *Jesus' Name is above all others.* "Wherefore God also hath highly exalted him, and given him a name which is above every name" (Philippians 2:9, KJV).

C. *Jesus is alive, and so is His Name.* "...Fear not; I am the first and the last: I am he that liveth, and was dead; and, behold, I am alive for evermore, Amen; and have the keys of hell and of death" (Revelation 1:17-18, KJV).

D. *Jesus has all authority.* "Then, Jesus came to them and said, 'All authority in heaven and on earth has been given to me'" (Matthew 28:18).

VII.   Now Go—in His Name!
"'And these signs will accompany those who believe: In my name they will drive out demons; they will speak in new tongues; they will pick up snakes with their hands; and when they drink deadly poison, it will not hurt them at all; they will place their hands on sick people, and they will get well.' After the Lord Jesus had spoken to them, he was taken up into heaven and he sat at the right hand of God. Then the disciples went out and preached

everywhere, and the Lord worked with them and confirmed his word by the signs that accompanied it'" (Mark 16:17-20).

All authority of God is in the Name of Jesus in the heavens and the earth, and His Name shows forth Him!

How to Locate the Enemy

I. **How to "See" With Your Spirit**

A. *Your human spirit (that part of you that is born again as in 1 Corinthians 6:17) is in union with God.*
   1. One Spirit. "But he who unites himself with the Lord is one with him in spirit" (1 Corinthians 6:17).
   2. You are the light. "Ye are the light of the world" (Matthew 5:14a, KJV).

B. *Believe you are in the Spirit.*
   1. Controlled by the Spirit. "You, however, are controlled not by the sinful nature but by the Spirit, if the Spirit of God lives in you" (Romans 8:9a).
   2. Do not rehearse doubt by saying that you fail to hear God.
   3. Do not be afraid of making a mistake.

C. *Know the operation of your spirit.*
   1. It knows every thought within. "For who among men knows the thoughts of a man except the man's spirit within him?" (1 Corinthians 2:11a)
   2. It always hears from the Holy Spirit. "...No one knows the thoughts of God except the Spirit of God. We have not received the spirit of the world but the

Spirit who is from God, that we may understand what God has freely given us" (1 Corinthians 2:11, 12).

3. It spiritually discerns (examines, scrutinizes, and investigates). "The man without the Spirit does not accept the things that come from the Spirit of God, for they are foolishness to him, and he cannot understand them, because they are spiritually discerned. The spiritual man makes judgments about all things, but he himself is not subject to any man's judgment: 'For who has known the mind of the Lord that he may instruct him?' But we have the mind of Christ" (1 Corinthians 2:14-16).

4. It knows true wisdom. "The wisdom that comes from heaven is first of all pure; then peace loving, considerate, submissive, full of mercy and good fruit, impartial and sincere" (James 3:17).

5. It is not double-minded. "But let him ask in faith, nothing wavering. For he that wavereth is like a wave of the sea driven with the wind and tossed. For let not that man think that he shall receive any thing of the Lord. A double minded man is unstable in all his ways" (James 1:6-8, KJV).

6. It is gentle and quiet. "...A gentle and quiet spirit, which is of great worth in God's sight" (1 Peter 3:4).

7. It receives gifts of the Spirit.
   a. Word of Knowledge
   b. Discerning (seeing) of Spirits
   c. Gift of Faith

8. It keeps you from the enemy. "We know that whosoever is born of God sinneth not; but he that is begotten of God keepeth himself, and that wicked

one toucheth him not" (1 John 5:18, KJV).

D. *Capture the thoughts of God.*
   1. Keep thoughts under control. "We demolish arguments and every pretension that sets itself up against the knowledge of God, and we take captive every thought to make it obedient to Christ" (2 Corinthians 10:5).
   2. Drop religious taboo ideas contrary to the Word of God. "Such regulations indeed have an appearance of wisdom, with their self-imposed worship, their false humility and their harsh treatment of the body, but they lack any value in restraining sensual indulgence" (Colossians 2:23).
   3. Do not judge by sight. "And there shall come forth a rod out of the stem of Jesse, and a Branch shall grow out of his roots: And the spirit of the LORD shall rest upon him, the spirit of wisdom and understanding, the spirit of counsel and might, the spirit of knowledge and of the fear of the LORD; And shall make him of quick understanding in the fear of the LORD: and he shall not judge after the sight of his eyes, neither reprove after the hearing of his ears: But with righteousness shall he judge the poor, and reprove with equity for the meek of the earth: and he shall smite the earth with the rod of his mouth, and with the breath of his lips shall he slay the wicked. And righteousness shall be the girdle of his loins, and faithfulness the girdle of his reins" (Isaiah 11:1-5, KJV).
      a. Receive spiritual edification. "He that speaketh

in an unknown tongue edifieth himself" (1 Corinthians 14:4a, KJV). "But ye, beloved, building up yourselves on your most holy faith, praying in the Holy Ghost" (Jude 1:20, KJV).

b. Receive interpretation. "Wherefore let him that speaketh in an unknown tongue pray that he may interpret" (1 Corinthians 14:13, KJV).

II. How to Identify, Locate, and Eradicate

A. *Be aggressive in the Holy Spirit.*

B. *Basic steps for locating the enemy's operation.*
1. Listen to people and use the four sources of wisdom or knowledge for identification.
   a. Human reason
   b. Flesh
   c. Satan and/or demons
   d. Holy Spirit
2. Line up people with the Word.
3. Examine "door openers."
4. Has the person repented, or is he still involved with the enemy?
5. Is he submitting to God's will?
6. Is he actively resisting Satan?
7. In the natural you may see depression, confusion, or fear on the face of the person. This is not always accurate.
8. What are you hearing in your spirit?
9. Ask the person what the Lord is showing him in his

spirit.

10. Get the person to pray in tongues with you before casting out, if possible.

11. You do not have to know a spirit's name to cast it out—only the area of involvement.

12. Recognize that it *does* take the Holy Spirit to work with you. "But if I drive out demons by the Spirit of God, then the kingdom of God has come upon you" (Matthew 12:28).

13. Never assume anything is a spirit: *Know.*

14. Follow Jesus' example: hear, see, and do! "...The Son can do nothing of himself, but what he seeth the Father do: for what things soever he doeth, these also doeth the Son likewise" (John 5:19, KJV).

Your Weapons against the Enemy

Name of Jesus

"Through thee will we push down our enemies" (Psalm 44:5a, KJV).

"And these signs will accompany those who believe: in my name they will drive out demons..." (Mark 16:17).

"...In the name of Jesus Christ I command you to come out of her!" (Acts 16:18).

Blood of Jesus

"And they overcame him by the blood of the Lamb, and by the word of their testimony; and they loved not their lives unto the death" (Revelation 12:11, KJV).

The Word of God

"But he [Jesus] answered [the devil] and said, It is written, Man shall not live by bread alone, but by every word that proceedeth out of the mouth of God. Jesus said unto him, It is written again, Thou shalt not tempt the Lord thy God. Then saith Jesus unto him, Get thee hence, Satan: for it is written, Thou shalt worship the Lord thy God, and him only shalt thou serve" (Matthew 4:4, 7, 10; KJV).

Armor

"...Let us put aside the deeds of darkness and put on the armor of light" (Romans 13:12).

"By the word of truth, by the power of God, by the armour of righteousness on the right hand and on the left" (2 Corinthians 6:7, KJV).

"Put on the full armor of God" (see Ephesians 6:11-17).

God's Ability, Authority, and Power in Us

"When Jesus had called the Twelve together, he gave them power and authority to drive out all demons and to cure diseases" (Luke 9:1).

"...Even the devils are subject unto us through thy name" (Luke 10:17, KJV).

"Behold, I give unto you power to tread on serpents and scorpions, and over all the power of the enemy: and nothing shall by any means hurt you" (Luke 10:19, KJV).

"But if I drive out demons by the Spirit of God, then the kingdom of God has come upon you" (Matthew 12:28).

"But ye shall receive power, after that the Holy Ghost is come upon you" (Acts 1:8a, KJV).

"The weapons we fight with are not the weapons of this world. On the contrary, they have divine power to demolish strongholds" (2 Corinthians 10:4).

"For he has rescued us from the dominion of darkness and brought us into the kingdom of the Son he loves" (Colossians 1:13)

"And having disarmed the powers and authorities, he made a public spectacle of them, triumphing over them by the cross" (Colossians 2:15)

"Finally, be strong in the Lord and in his mighty power" (Ephesians 6:10).

"Which he wrought in Christ, when he raised him from the dead, and set him at his own right hand in the heavenly places, Far above all principality, and power, and might, and dominion, and every name that is named, not only in this world, but also in that which is to come" (Ephesians 1:20-21, KJV).

"Who is gone into heaven, and is on the right hand of God; angels and authorities and powers being made subject unto" (1 Peter 3:22, KJV).

"...That by his death he might destroy him who holds the power of death—that is, the devil" (Hebrews 2:14).

"And God raised us up with Christ and seated us with him in the heavenly realms in Christ Jesus" (Ephesians 2:6).

"...The one who is in you is greater than the one who is in the world" (1 John 4:4).

"...The yoke shall be destroyed because of the anointing" (Isaiah 10:27, KJV).

"The Spirit of the Lord is upon me, because he hath anointed me to preach the gospel to the poor; he hath sent me to heal the brokenhearted, to preach deliverance to the captives, and recovering of sight to the blind, to set at liberty them that are bruised" (Luke 4:18, KJV).

How to Win Every Battle

Follow these guidelines when encountering evil spirits:

I. Be sensitive to the Spirit of God

A. *Revealed by God.* "Jesus replied, 'Blessed are you, Simon son of Jonah, for this was not revealed to you by man, but by my Father in heaven. And I tell you that you are Peter, and on this rock I will build my church, and the gates of Hades will not overcome it. I will give you the keys of the kingdom of heaven; whatever you bind on earth will be bound in heaven, and whatever you loose on earth will be loosed in heaven'" (Matthew 16:17-19).

B. *Satan will try to trick you so you will ask, "What's in it for me?"*

II. Be Firm and Constant In God's Promises

A. *"Be sober, be vigilant;* because your adversary the devil, as a roaring lion, walketh about, seeking whom he may devour: Whom resist stedfast in the faith, knowing that the same afflictions are accomplished in your brethren that are in the world" (1 Peter 5:8-9, KJV).

B. *"That ye be not slothful,* but followers of them who through faith and patience inherit the promises" (Hebrews 6:12, KJV).

III. Confront Boldly with Authority

"And to make all men see what is the fellowship of the mystery, which from the beginning of the world hath been hid in God, who created all things by Jesus Christ: To the intent that now unto the principalities and powers in heavenly places might be known by the church the manifold wisdom of God, According to the eternal purpose which he purposed in Christ Jesus our Lord: In whom we have boldness and access with confidence by the faith of him" (Ephesians 3:9-12, KJV).

IV. Bind the Spirit in Jesus' Name

A. *Bind to restrict the demon's activity so the casting out is far less violent.*

B. *Bind the spirit from manifesting and speaking.*

C. *Bind the strong man and spoil his goods.* "No man can enter into a strong man's house, and spoil his goods, except he will first bind the strong man; and then he will spoil his house" (Mark 3:27, KJV).

D. *Bind their kings.* "To bind their kings with chains, and their nobles with fetters of iron; To execute upon them the judgment written: this honour have all his saints. Praise ye the LORD" (Psalm 149:8-9, KJV).

E. *Bind on earth.* "Jesus replied, 'Blessed are you, Simon son of Jonah, for this was not revealed to you by man, but by my Father in heaven. And I tell you that you are Peter, and on this rock I will build my church, and the gates of Hades will not over come it. I will give you the keys of the kingdom of heaven; whatever you bind on earth will be bound in heaven, and whatever you loose on earth will be loosed in heaven'" (Matthew 16:17-19).

"Verily I say unto you, Whatsoever ye shall bind on earth shall be bound in heaven: and whatsoever ye shall loose on earth shall be loosed in heaven. Again I say unto you, That if two of you shall agree on earth as touching any thing that they shall ask, it shall be done for them of my Father which is in heaven. For where two or three are gathered together in my name, there am I in the midst of them" (Matthew 18:18-20, KJV).

V. Command the Demonic Spirit to Come out in Jesus' Name

A. *Paul said, "...In the name of Jesus Christ I command you to come out of her..."* (Acts 16:18).

B. *Exercise authority, not knowledge or arguments.* Demons hear authority, not volume.

C. *Cast out devils.* "And these signs will accompany those who believe: In my name they will drive out demons;

they will speak in new tongues" (Mark 16:17).

D. *Cast down imaginations.* "We demolish arguments and every pretension that sets itself up against the knowledge of God, and we take captive every thought to make it obedient to Christ" (2 Corinthians 10:5).

VI. Resist Actively and Aggressively
"Submit yourselves therefore to God. Resist the devil, and he will flee from you" (James 4:7, KJV).

VII. Wrestle, Not as an Equal Opposite
"For our struggle is not against flesh and blood, but against the rulers, against the authorities, against the powers of this dark world and against the spiritual forces of evil in the heavenly realms" (Ephesians 6:12).

VIII. Pull Down the Strongholds
"The weapons we fight with are not weapons of the world. On the contrary, they have divine power to demolish strongholds" (2 Corinthians 10:4).

IX. Stand Firm and Immovable against the Enemy

A. *Ability to stand.* "Put on the full armor of God so that you can take your stand against the devil's schemes" (Ephesians 6:11).

B. *Having done all, stand.* "Therefore put on the full armor of God, so that when the day of evil comes, you may be able to stand your ground, and after you have done everything, to stand" (Ephesians 6:13).

X.   Protect Yourself

A. *Keep yourself.* "We know that anyone born of God does not continue to sin; the one who was born of God keeps him safe, and the evil one cannot harm him" (1 John 5:18).

B. *Give no place.*
   1. Once you become spiritually alert, Satan cannot enter your life unless you give him opportunity. "Neither give place to the devil" (Ephesians 4:27, KJV).

XI.   Use the Word

A. *It is written!* "But he answered and said, It is written, Man shall not live by bread alone, but by every word that proceedeth out of the mouth of God. Jesus said unto him, It is written again, Thou shalt not tempt the Lord thy God. Then saith Jesus unto him, Get thee hence, Satan: for it is written, Thou shalt worship the Lord thy God, and him only shalt thou serve" (Matthew 4:4, 7, 10, KJV).

B. *The wisdom of God preached to the devil and spirits.* "To the intent that now unto the principalities and powers in heavenly places might be known by the church the manifold wisdom of God, According to the eternal purpose which he purposed in Christ Jesus our Lord: In whom we have boldness and access with confidence by the faith of him" (Ephesians 3:10-12, KJV).

C. *Preach to the devil about the power of the blood.* "And they overcame him by the blood of the Lamb, and by the word of their testimony; and they loved not their lives unto the death" (Revelation 12:11, KJV).

XII. Praise the Lord

A. *Put on the garment of praise.* "And provide for those who grieve in Zion—to bestow on them a crown of beauty instead of ashes, the oil of gladness instead of mourning, and a garment of praise instead of a spirit of despair. They will be called oaks of righteousness, a planting of the Lord for the display of his splendor" (Isaiah 61:3).

B. *God inhabits praise.* "But thou art holy, O thou that inhabitest the praises of Israel" (Psalm 22:3, KJV).

C. *Saul was delivered when David sang.* (See 1 Samuel 16:14-23).

D. *Jehoshaphat sang out praises; God sent ambushments.* "And when he had consulted with the people, he appointed singers unto the LORD, and that should praise the beauty of holiness, as they went out before the army, and to say, Praise the LORD; for his mercy endureth for ever. And when they began to sing and to praise, the LORD set ambushments against the children of Ammon, Moab, and mount Seir, which were come against Judah; and they were smitten" (2 Chronicles 20:21-22, KJV).

XIII. Pray and Fast

A. "He [Jesus] replied, 'This kind can come out only by prayer [some manuscripts add *and fasting*'" (Mark 9:29).

B. *God's chosen fast.* "Is not this the fast that I have chosen? to loose the bands of wickedness, to undo the heavy burdens, and to let the oppressed go free, and that ye break every yoke?" (Isaiah 58:6, KJV).
   1. To loose the bands of wickedness
   2. To undo the heavy burdens
   3. To let the oppressed go free
   4. To break every yoke

XIV. Break Evil Words

A. *The Word is sharper than any two-edged sword.* "For the word of God is living and active. Sharper than any double-edge sword, it penetrates even to dividing soul and spirit, joints and marrow; it judges the thoughts and attitudes of the heart" (Hebrews 4:12).

B. *We break other swords.* (See Psalm 64.)

C. *Condemn judgmental words.* "No weapon that is formed

against thee shall prosper; and every tongue that shall rise against thee in judgment thou shalt condemn. This is the heritage of the servants of the LORD, and their righteousness is of me, saith the LORD" (Isaiah 54:17, KJV).

XV.   Do Not Ever Quit in Spiritual Warfare!

A. *Remember, it is not over until you have won!* "...We have heard with our ears, O God, our fathers have told us, what work thou didst in their days, in the times of old. How thou didst drive out the heathen with thy hand, and plantedst them; how thou didst afflict the people, and cast them out. For they got not the land in possession by their own sword, neither did their own arm save them: but thy right hand, and thine arm, and the light of thy countenance, because thou hadst a favour unto them. Thou art my King, O God: command deliverances for Jacob. Through thee will we push down our enemies: through thy name will we tread them under that rise up against us. For I will not trust in my bow, neither shall my sword save me. But thou hast saved us from our enemies, and hast put them to shame that hated us. In God we boast all the day long, and praise thy name for ever. Selah" (Psalm 44:1-8, KJV).

Part 5

Appendix

Contents

How to Receive God's Free Gift

Have you ever received God's free gift of Eternal Life? Do you know for certain that if you were to die today you would go to Heaven? Everlasting life is a gift from God. When Jesus Christ died on the cross and rose bodily from the grave, He paid for our sins. The Bible says:

> For God so loved the world, that he gave his only begotten Son, that whosoever believeth in him should not perish, but have everlasting life.
>
> John 3:16 (KJV)

Since Jesus paid for this gift, we don't have to. We only need to receive it.

> But as many as received him, to them gave he power to become the sons of God, even to them that believe on his name.
>
> John 1:12 (KJV)

> For by grace are ye saved through faith; and that not of yourselves: it is the gift of God:
> Not of works, lest any man should boast.
>
> Ephesians 2:8-9 (KJV)

The way to receive God's gift simply is to believe God's Word and receive it by the profession of your mouth.

257

That if you confess with your mouth, "Jesus is Lord," and believe in your heart that God raised him from the dead, you will be saved.

For it is with your heart that you believe and are justified, and it is with your mouth that you confess and are saved.

Romans 10:9-10

Now, pray this prayer aloud:

Father, thank You for loving me. Thank You for giving Your Son, Jesus, to die for me.

Jesus Christ, Son of God, come into my heart, forgive me of my sins, and be my Lord and Savior. Jesus, I declare that You are Lord, and that You are Lord of my life. In Jesus' Name. Amen.

You are now born again!

All believers are entitled to over 7,000 promises that God has written in His Word. That now includes you! To learn about these promises, attend church regularly. If you are in the area of New Castle, Delaware, please join us for services at Victory Christian Fellowship. Visit our web site at www.gwwm.com for directions and more information. I encourage you to attend a local church that teaches the uncompromised Word of God— the Bible. Daily spend time in prayer, fellowship with the Lord, and reading the Bible. This will help you to understand the "new creature" that you have become now in Christ.

...If any man be in Christ, he is a *new creature:* old things are passed away; behold, all things are become new.

2 Corinthians 5:17 (KJV)

For more information about your new life in Christ, please order *The Victorious Walk* book. *Purchase this book wherever fine Christian products are sold in your area. Or, see the product list and order form at the back of this book.*

Have You Received the Holy Spirit Since You Believed?

In Acts 19:2 (NKJV), the apostle Paul asked the Ephesians this very important question:

"Did you receive the Holy Spirit when you believed?"

The question startled them, and they answered:

"We have not so much as heard whether there is a Holy Spirit."

Later, when they prayed together:

...The Holy Spirit came on them, and they spoke in tongues and prophesied.

Acts 19:6

What Is the Baptism in the Holy Spirit?

The Baptism in the Holy Spirit is an anointing of power, an enabling or ability from God in the believer's life, which equips him or her to witness fully of the life of Jesus Christ.

The Holy Spirit was given on the Day of Pentecost and has never left. This is a distinct experience from conversion to Christ. The Baptism in the Holy Spirit was a separate experience in Jesus' life when He was water baptized, in the apostles' lives on the Day of Pentecost, and in the believer's life today.

Who Is It for, and What Is It?

The Baptism in the Holy Spirit is for believers, because the world cannot receive Him. This experience is to equip and empower believers to worship God supernaturally. The first move of the Holy Spirit when He came upon the early Christians was to speak the praises of God through them (Acts 2:11).

This Baptism is God's outpouring of His Spirit into a person's life to equip him or her to be a witness of Jesus. Christ said:

> But ye shall receive power, after that the Holy Ghost is come upon you: and ye shall be witnesses unto me both in Jerusalem, and in all Judaea, and in Samaria, and unto the uttermost part of the earth.
>
> Acts 1:8 (KJV)

Why Be Baptized in the Holy Spirit?

It is God's will for every believer to be baptized in the Holy Spirit. It is His desire that you overflow with His Spirit continually. Jesus COMMANDED the disciples not to leave Jerusalem until they had been endued with power.

> And, behold, I send the promise of my Father upon you: but tarry ye in the city of Jerusalem, until ye be endued with power from on high.
>
> Luke 24:49 (KJV)

In Ephesians 5:17-18, the Word of God says that believers

261

are to understand (comprehend, grasp, perceive) what the will of the Lord is. Also, they are to be filled with the Holy Spirit.

> Wherefore be ye not unwise, but understanding what the will of the Lord is.
> And be not drunk with wine, wherein is excess; but be filled with the Spirit.
> Ephesians 5:17-18 (KJV)

Jesus also said those who believe on Him SHOULD receive the Holy Spirit:

> (But this spake he of the Spirit, which they that believe on him should receive: for the Holy Ghost was not yet given; because that Jesus was not yet glorified.)
> John 7:39 (KJV)

How Do I Receive the Baptism in the Holy Spirit?

Ask and you will receive. Knowing that it is God's will for us to be filled with the Holy Spirit gives us confidence in asking Him to baptize us in the Holy Spirit.

> And this is the confidence that we have in him, that, if we ask any thing according to his will, he heareth us:
> ...If we know that he hear us, whatsoever we ask, we know that we have the petitions that we desired of him.
> 1 John 5:14-15 (KJV)

> ...Ask, and it shall be given you...
> ...how much more shall your heavenly Father give

the Holy Spirit to them that ask him?

Luke 11:9, 13 (KJV)

What Happens when I Receive this Baptism?

New Language

One of the first experiences that we have when we are filled with the Holy Spirit is that God gives to us a supernatural language. Our hearts are turned more completely to God, to whom we were reconciled already in Jesus Christ when we were born again. Jesus said:

> And these signs shall follow them that believe...they shall speak with new tongues.

Mark 16:17 (KJV)

The Gentiles in the house of Cornelius spoke with tongues when the Holy Spirit came on them (Acts 10:44-48). Likewise, as we studied earlier, the people of Ephesus spoke in tongues when the Holy Spirit came upon them:

> And when Paul had laid hands on them, the Holy Spirit came upon them, and they spoke with tongues and prophesied.

Acts 19:6 (NKJV)

What Does Speaking in Tongues Do?

Praises the Lord in a God-Appointed Way

> ...When thou shalt bless with the spirit...
> ...thou verily givest thanks well....

1 Corinthians 14:16-17 (KJV)

Edifies Spiritually

He that speaketh in an unknown tongue edifieth himself.

1 Corinthians 14:4a (KJV)

Reminds of the Holy Spirit's Indwelling Presence

"And I will pray the Father, and He will give you another Helper, that He may abide with you forever,

"even the Spirit of truth, whom the world cannot receive, because it neither sees Him nor knows Him; but you know Him, for He dwells with you and will be in you."

John 14:16-17 (NKJV)

Prays in Line with God's Perfect Will

Likewise the Spirit also helpeth our infirmities: for we know not what we should pray for as we ought: but the Spirit itself maketh intercession for us with groanings which cannot be uttered.

And he that searcheth the hearts knoweth what is the mind of the Spirit, because he maketh intercession for the saints according to the will of God.

Romans 8:26-27 (KJV)

Stimulates Faith

But ye, beloved, building up yourselves on your most holy faith, praying in the Holy Ghost.

Jude 1:20 (KJV)

Appendix

Refreshes Spiritually

For with stammering lips and another tongue will he speak to this people.

To whom he said, This is the rest wherewith ye may cause the weary to rest; and this is the refreshing: yet they would not hear.

Isaiah 28:11-12 (KJV)

Opens Your Prayer Line to God

For he that speaketh in an unknown tongue speaketh not unto men, but unto God: for no man understandeth him; howbeit in the spirit he speaketh mysteries.

For if I pray in an unknown tongue, my spirit prayeth, but my understanding is unfruitful.

1 Corinthians 14:2, 14 (KJV)

Please pray this prayer aloud now:

Father, thank You that at the moment I ask to be filled with the Holy Spirit, I will be filled. The evidence is that I will speak with other tongues by my will, though I will not understand with my mind. Now, Father, fill me with the Holy Spirit, in the Name of Jesus. Thank You for filling me. I have received, now. By a decision of my will, I speak to You in other tongues. In Jesus' Name. Amen.

We can build ourselves up and speak to God wherever we are—in the car, riding the bus or airplane, at home, or on the job. It will not disturb anyone. Speaking in tongues is a means of

265

keeping free from the contamination of the world.

Supernatural Gifts of Power

The gifts of the Holy Spirit can begin now to operate in and through your life. According to 1 Corinthians 12:7-11, the nine gifts of the Spirit are:

- Word of Wisdom
- Word of Knowledge
- Discerning of Spirits
- Prophecy
- Diversity of Tongues
- Interpretation of Tongues
- Special Faith
- Healings
- Working of Miracles

For more information about how to live as a victorious Christian, please order *The Victorious Walk* book. *Purchase this book wherever fine Christian products are sold in your area. Or, see the product list and order form at the back of this book.*

Notes

Chapter 7

[1] W.E. Vine, M.A., *Vine's Expository Dictionary of New Testament Words Unabridged Edition* (Peabody: Hendrickson Publishers), p. 293.

Chapter 10

[1] Joseph Henry Thayer, D.D., *Thayer's Greek-English Lexicon of the New Testament* (Marshallton: The National Foundation for Christian Education), p. 124.

Chapter 13

[1] *The American Heritage® Dictionary of the English Language, Third Edition* (Houghton Mifflin Company, electronic version licensed from INSO Corporation).

Products by Gary V. Whetstone

Purchase the following products where Christian products are sold in your area. Or order using the form at the end of this book.

Freedom Series

Assignment Against the Church: The Spirit of Offense
The demonic stronghold of the Prince of Offense and his diabolical plan to cripple the Body of Christ is exposed and dealt with in this life-changing tape series.

| | 6-tape audio | $ 35.00 | VR001A |

Blood-Bought Promises
Understand the awesome covenant that God has with you through the Blood of Jesus. These tapes provide a complete understanding of the terms, provision, and power of the covenant. Hold onto your seat...you never will relate to God or His provisions in the same way again!

| Includes study guide | 4-tape audio | $ 25.00 | VR002A |
| | 4-hour video | $ 50.00 | VR002V |

Discovering God's Highway to Your Destiny
God has an awesome plan for your life. The revelations that you will receive from this series will be life-changing as you travel on His expressway.

| Includes study guide | 4-tape audio | $ 25.00 | VE006A |

Extracting the Gold from Life's Crises
Learn how to correctly handle pressure, stress, conflict, and temptation so they work for your benefit! This series will teach you how to draw the wealth out of distresses in life by going THROUGH them in victory.

| Includes study guide | 4-tape audio | $ 25.00 | VR003A |
| | 4-hour video | $ 50.00 | VR003V |

Fire Storm
Learn how to build your protective prayer wall.

| | 2-tape audio | $ 13.00 | VR018T |

Freedom from Insecurity and Inferiority —
Crowned to Reign as a King
Do you struggle with insecurities and feelings of inferiority? Do the memories of your past seem to limit your future potential? This series will help you to experience freedom to reign as a king over your perceived limitations.

| Includes study guide | 6-tape audio | $ 35.00 | VR004A |
| | 6-hour video | $ 75.00 | VR004V |

How to Harness Your Mind
The mind of man with all its complexities and conflicts can indeed be

harnessed and put to good use to serve the Lord. This series discusses the four sources of wisdom the mind receives, how to change the way you think, mental warfare, and possessing the mind of Christ.

Includes study guide   4-tape audio $ 25.00   VR011A

How to Stop Satan's Attack on God's Timing, Plans and Purposes

This course is an extraordinary, behind-the-scenes exposé of how Satan interferes with God's will for your life. Biblically, you will study the predestinated purpose, plan, and timing already set by God for you. Learn why these areas may not be working and how to stop the enemy "dead in his tracks."

Includes study guide   9-tape audio $ 45.00   BM203A00

How to Identify and Remove Curses!

Unseen words spoken by you or others have restricted and limited your success in life. This series helps you to break the power of the curses that are working against you.

ISBN 0-9664462-1-6   Book (English) $ 8.00   VR005B
ISBN 0-9664462-5-9   Book (Spanish) $ 9.00   VR005P
Includes study guide   6-tape audio $ 35.00   VR005A
*   6-hour video $ 75.00   VR005V*

The Journey from Frustration to Fulfillment

Are you living in frustration—knowing that God has a plan, purpose, and destiny in store for you but not yet fulfilling it? This series reveals how to remove the restrictions that have thwarted God's destiny for your life and gives an action plan that will lift you to a new level of purpose, excitement, and fulfillment in your life.

Includes study guide   6-tape audio $ 35.00   VR006A

Love's Transforming Power

God's love for us is awesome. This series will anchor you in the revelation of God's love that will transform you to become secure, moldable, and pliable in God's hands every moment of your life.

Includes study guide   4-tape audio $ 25.00   VR007A
*   4-hour video $ 50.00   VR007V*

Make Fear Bow

Experience an understanding of the causes of your fears that will enable you to break free from their bondage so you can live victoriously in God's promises.

ISBN 0-9664462-3-2   Paperback Book $ 8.00   VR008B
Includes study guide   4-tape audio $ 25.00   VR008A

The Power of the Lord's Blessing

Many believers are not experiencing God's blessing. This series reveals how to free yourself from Satan's barriers of frustration and self-effort. Break through to the blessings God has destined for you.

Includes study guide   4-tape audio $ 25.00   VR009A

Victory in Spiritual Warfare
This engaging and informative, yet shocking, revelation presents a comprehensive, biblical explanation of spiritual warfare, and teaches a practical and effective strategy for overcoming the work of evil spirits. Once the light of revelation comes, you will be able to identify, locate, and eradicate the power of the enemy.

8-tape audio	$ 45.00	VR010A
8-hour video	$ 99.00	VR010V

Conquering Your Unseen Enemies	*Book (English)*	$ 12.99	VR013B
Conquering Your Unseen Enemies	*Book (Spanish)*	$ 12.99	VR014B

Victory in Spiritual Warfare Seminar
For those interested in further study of God's Word on identifying, locating, and destroying the works of darkness, this detailed, in-depth course, offered as a follow-up to the School of Victorious Living 8-tape *Victory in Spiritual Warfare* series, will fully equip you to live above every attack and plan of the enemy.

Includes study guide	*26-tape audio*	$125.00	BM201A00
Study guide		$ 13.00	BM103500

The Victorious Walk
This book covers the basic, foundational truths that are necessary for every believer to live victoriously.

ISBN 0-9664462-0-8	*Book (English)*	$ 3.00	VE021B
ISBN 0-9664462-9-1	*Book (Spanish)*	$ 3.00	VE022B

Radio and TV Broadcasts

**Gary Whetstone Worldwide Ministries
also reaches out daily across
parts of the United States
on radio and television**

**Call for the broadcast schedule
in your region: 1 (302) 324-5400**

Or visit our web site at *www.gwwm.com* ...
- **Tune in to our daily radio programs**
- **Watch our TV programming**
- **Search our online product catalog**
- **View our Bible School course descriptions**

Dig Deeper in Christ with these
Life-Changing Books by Gary Whetstone

The following books are available wherever Christian products are sold in your area. Or order using the product catalog and form on our web site at *www.gwwm.com* or at the back of this book. Currently, these paperback books are available in various foreign languages or will be soon. Contact us for more information.

How to Identify and Remove Curses!

What you don't know *can* hurt you. Today, many Christians suffer unnecessary defeat, because they are unaware of their enemy's subtle tactics. This book provides practical, biblical steps to recognize and break unseen curses that could be holding you captive and destroying your life. Get ready for the Holy Spirit to set you free!

English	ISBN 0-9664462-1-6	VR005B	$8.00
Spanish	ISBN 0-9664462-5-9	VR005P	$9.00

Conquering Your Unseen Enemies

English	ISBN 0-9664462-2-4	VR013B	$12.99
Spanish	ISBN 0-9664462-6-7	VR014B	$12.99

The Victorious Walk

English	ISBN 0-9664462-0-8	VE021B	$ 3.00
Spanish	ISBN 0-9664462-9-1	VE022B	$ 3.00

Life's Answers
ISBN, Stock Number, and Price to be announced

Make Fear Bow
ISBN, Stock Number, and Price to be announced

It Only Takes One
ISBN, Stock Number, and Price to be announced

Millionaire Mentality
ISBN, Stock Number, and Price to be announced

Gary Whetstone Worldwide Ministries
P.O. Box 10050 • Wilmington, DE 19850 U.S.A.
PHONE: 1 (302) 324-5400
FAX: 1 (302) 324-5448
WEB SITE: www.gwwm.com
E-MAIL: info@gwwm.com

Pastor Gary invites you to:

Victory Christian Fellowship

One of the Fastest-Growing Churches on the U.S. East Coast!

SERVICE SCHEDULE

Sunday Morning	8:30 a.m.	Worship & Teaching
	11:00 a.m.	Worship & Teaching
Sunday Evening	6:00 p.m.	Water Baptism
	7:00 p.m.	Worship & Teaching
Wednesday	7:00 p.m.	Worship & Teaching

This church is dedicated to reaching out to meet your family's needs and to help you grow strong spiritually through the revelation knowledge of God's Word. Your faith will be strengthened as you see that Word in action! Visit today or call for prayer.

VICTORY CHRISTIAN FELLOWSHIP
100 Wilton Blvd.
New Castle, DE 19720   U.S.A.
PHONE: 1 (302) 324-5400
FAX: 1 (302) 324-5448
WEB SITE: www.gwwm.com
E-MAIL: info@gwwm.com

(On Rte. 40, just past the 13/40 split at Wilton.)

Pastor Gary V. Whetstone

What will you do with God's call on your life?

Find God's Answer Through:

School of Victorious Living

Face life's challenges with proven biblical answers!

Audio/video teachings with study guides available for study in your own home.

School of Biblical Studies

Establish a closer relationship with God!
Gain a deeper understanding of His Word.

An in-depth bible school curriculum for the serious student of God's Word.

School of Ministerial Training

Called into full-time ministry?
Pastor/Teacher · Evangelist/Missionary
Church Helps · Music Ministry

Receive hands-on training along with classroom instruction.

Gary Whetstone

Gary Whetstone is the Senior Pastor and Founder of Victory Christian Fellowship in New Castle, Delaware, and Founder of Gary Whetstone Worldwide Ministries. He earned his Doctor of Religious Education degree from Chesapeake Bible College and Seminary in Ridgely, Maryland.

Since personally experiencing God's miraculous deliverance and healing in 1971, Gary Whetstone has devoted his life to helping others become free. He ministers locally, nationally, and internationally in evangelistic crusades and to equip the Body of Christ for victory in spiritual warfare. Gifted in teaching, Gary Whetstone provides sound, biblical instruction and practical strategy for defeating the enemy in every area of life.

Through the local outreach of Victory Christian Fellowship, God has set free hundreds of thousands of people in salvations, Baptisms in the Holy Spirit, healings, and many other signs, wonders, and miracles. Having a great burden to minister to the local community, Pastor Gary Whetstone and his church have launched life-changing outreaches in several areas: HIV/AIDS; substance and alcohol abuse; inner-city community outreach centers; Saturday Sidewalk Sunday School; food and clothing outreach programs; and many large evangelistic campaigns, including dramatic productions such as "Jesus, Light of the World," which draws over 45,000 people annually.

Gary Whetstone's heart's desire is to see 1,000 missionaries placed on the mission field from his ministry. To accomplish that dream, he has established the School of Biblical Studies (a video Bible school) and the School of Ministerial Training. Currently, the video school has several hundred national and international locations, which were opened in cooperation with many local churches. Gary Whetstone also holds crusades internationally, which draw crowds of tens of thousands. For many, these crusades are their first opportunity to hear the Gospel of Jesus Christ. Pastor Gary also sends forth evangelism teams, which minister both locally and internationally.

Gary Whetstone has appeared on many national and international radio and television programs, and has authored key books, among which are *The Victorious Walk, How to Identify and Remove Curses!, Make Fear Bow, Millionaire Mentality*, and his personal testimony of miraculous deliverance and healing in *Conquering Your Unseen Enemies*. The large number of study guides he has produced are a testament to his gifting in practical biblical teaching and are available for use with his numerous video and audio teaching series.

God has gifted Pastor Gary Whetstone with an incredible business sense and ability, enabling him to publish a series of teachings from *Purchasing and Negotiations* to *Success in Business* and *Millionaire Mentality*, which has aired on his 14-year-long radio program, "Power Impact." This broadcast currently reaches an audience of over four million listeners on the East Coast of the United States.

Gary Whetstone and his wife, Faye, have a particularly dynamic testimony of a restored marriage, which achieved national attention and was the cover story in *Charisma* magazine. Gary and Faye now conduct annual Marriage Advance seminars for couples looking to deeply enrich their relationships.

Pastors Gary and Faye Whetstone recently celebrated their 26th wedding anniversary. Their two adult children, Eric and Laurie, along with daughter-in-law, Rebecca, and grandson, Isaiah, are involved actively in the local and international Whetstone ministry.

To arrange a speaking engagement for Gary or Faye Whetstone, please contact:

> Gary Whetstone Worldwide Ministries
> P.O. Box 10050
> Wilmington, DE 19850 U.S.A.
> PHONE: 1 (302) 324-5400
> FAX: 1 (302) 324-5448
> WEB SITE: www.gwwm.com
> E-MAIL: info@gwwm.com

Gary Whetstone Worldwide Ministries
Product and Information Order Form

☐ Rev.　　☐ Mr.　　☐ Mrs.　　☐ Ms.　　☐ Miss　　(Please print)

Name_____

Address_____

City_____ State_____ ZIP_____

Home Phone (_____)_____ Work Phone (_____)_____

E-mail_____

Please send information about the following to me:

    ☐ Ministry Products (Catalog)
    ☐ Gary Whetstone Worldwide Ministries (Information and Itinerary)
    ☐ School of Victorious Living (Audio/video teachings)
    ☐ School of Biblical Studies (Delaware campuses or out-of-state sites)
    ☐ School of Biblical Studies (Audio-correspondence program)
    ☐ School of Ministerial Training (Delaware campus)
    ☐ Victory Christian Fellowship (Church)

☐ **Pastor Gary, please pray for me. I am enclosing my prayer needs on a separate page.**

☐ **Pastor Gary, enclosed on a separate sheet is my testimony of how this book and/or your ministry ministered to me.**

Please send the following products to me:

Quantity	Item #	Title	Price	Total
			$	$
			$	$
			$	$
			$	$

(U.S.A.) SHIPPING & HANDLING		
Up to $10.00....$1.50	Subtotal	$
$10.01-$50.00...$3.50	Shipping/Handling	$
$50.01-Up.........$5.00	TOTAL	$

Credit Card: ☐MasterCard　☐VISA　☐American Express　☐Discover

Account No._____

Expiration Date_____

Signature_____

Please make all checks payable in U.S. Dollars to "G.W.W.M."
Allow 4-6 weeks for delivery. No C.O.D.'s accepted.

Send your order and payment to:
Gary Whetstone Worldwide Ministries
P.O. Box 10050 • Wilmington, DE 19850 U.S.A.
PHONE: 1 (302) 324-5400 • FAX: 1 (302) 324-5448 • WEB SITE: www.gwwm.com
E-MAIL: info@gwwm.com